DIANE MONIER-MOORE

For David Sellers,

DINAN
THE ENGLISH CEMETERY,

*" some corner of a foreign field
That is for ever England" ...*

*with my best wishes -
Diane .
8.6.18 .*

Editions Plessix

Published by:
Editions Plessix
St Jacut
La Route de Vinchelez
St Ouen
Jersey JE3 2DA
Great Britain

© Editions Plessix 2018

ISBN 978-0-9928048-4-8

Diane Monier-Moore
Editions Plessix
00 44 1534 481067
email: editionsplessix@gmail.com
Author's email: dianemoorejersey@yahoo.co.uk
Web: www.editionsplessix.com

**Cover photograph by Francis Cauwel: The araucaria tree in the *Cimetière anglais*,
Dinan, believed to have been planted by members of the English Colony 160 years ago
and can be regarded as a living legacy of those who rest in its shade.**

INTRODUCTION

This small publication is designed to complement my book, *Dinan – The English Colony: 1800-1940* and represents a photographic and biographical database of the English Cemetery in Dinan. The burial ground forms part not only of Dinan's heritage, but also that of those whose remains rest here; it can be looked upon as a living memorial to those who played a role in the English-speaking community of Dinan in the 19th Century, and this book seeks to highlight its importance as an historic site in a manner which was not fully possible in the context of a much larger work. It is hoped my readers might wish to explore the *Cimetière anglais* with this guidebook and visit the graves of those whose lives touched many.

As readers of my book will know, one of my principal sources of information is the 22-volume diary of an Anglo-Frenchman, Cosme de Satgé (1840-1898). He spent the last 15 years of his life in Dinan with his family, and he became acquainted with a significant number of those who, like him, his wife, mother and young sons, are also interred in the English Cemetery.

I frequently us the term "English" in spite of many individuals stemming from Irish, Scottish, Welsh and Channel Island origins. The residents of the Colony happily referred to themselves as "English" and used the term far more liberally than we would now, so I have continued to use the word in the hope that my readers will accept and understand the reasoning behind this. Their use of the label "English" actually suggests that it was the English language which united them rather than their place of birth.

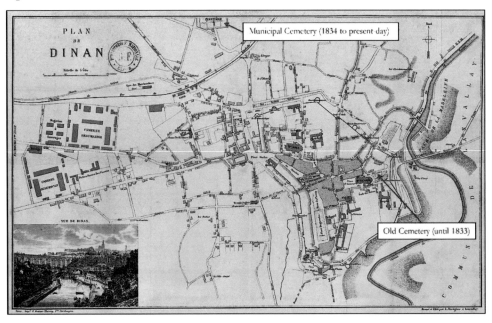

Map of Dinan in 1880. (*Coll. BnF*).

3

A New Cemetery

As a result of a number of contributing factors including epidemics, the French Revolution and lack of space in the only remaining inner-city cemetery (located behind the church of *Saint-Sauveur*), the town of Dinan finally opened its gates to a new communal cemetery located well outside the perimeter of the walled town on January 1st 1834. It is interesting to note that the old cemetery was later landscaped into a park based upon Napoleon III's love of English gardens; initially named the *Jardin de la Duchesse Anne* when it was opened around 1853, it was re-baptised the *Jardin anglais* towards the end of the nineteenth century in honour of the *Colonie anglaise*, The English Colony.

Plaque in the *Jardin anglais* at the site of the old cemetery.

The new cemetery expanded over the coming years and can be best described as being "cemeteries within the cemetery". As well as housing the remains of many locals in a microcosmic representation of Dinan through the ages, one can find within the grounds a significant military section (which unites French and German soldiers), a very moving children's cemetery, and what is still referred to today as *Le Cimetière anglais* or *Le Carré anglais* – both terms used interchangeably in written and spoken French. The entire cemetery is worthy of a visit; in a way no museum or library can ever replicate, it brings together in one place a whole host of people who all had some role to play in Dinan's history. The funerals of most of those who passed away after the inauguration of Christ Church Dinan in December 1870 took place inside this new place of worship.

Christ Church Dinan (*Coll. Bibliothèque municipale. de Dinan*).

The *Cimetière anglais* initially did not just unite the British Anglican residents of Dinan, but it also housed all Protestants, Lutherans, Calvinists and those of any non-Catholic faith irrespective of their nationality. We also find a number of French Catholics buried here too, as a law passed in 1881 stated that no separation of cults was needed in places of burial. This has led to the removal of a number of Protestant graves where British people once rested and even in more modern times, graves whose leases expired have been replaced by new random graves. Over thirty British graves have been lost.

An Endangered Legacy

It is not just development which is a concern; it is abandonment. Many of the Britons' graves are falling into rack and ruin because no descendants are there to tend to them. In most cases, any descendants are untraceable. The stones are covered in moss, some are broken, the inscriptions are barely legible, the ground is sinking and at this rate part of the *Colonie*'s heritage will be lost within the next fifty years. At least 25 graves are seriously endangered. It is hoped that this guidebook will encourage public figures and individuals alike to contribute either financially or physically towards the conservation of this valuable part of our history. *Editions Plessix*, publishers of this text, will be donating some of the proceeds of this guidebook towards the preservation and restoration of the English Cemetery

It is not an unrealistic project. Over the last three years I have had to remove moss and layers of mud from many of the gravestones and slabs in order to decipher inscriptions and find clues as to the identities of those resting beneath. With an enthusiastic team of volunteers, we could continue this work along with the assistance of professionals, and in the case of the most deteriorated graves, their equipment.

The pages which follow tell the story of those who rest in the English Cemetery. I have remained faithful to the numbering shown on the most recent plans held by the *Ville de Dinan*, although any errors have been corrected. The original section of the cemetery starts at 1A as can be seen on the charts. However, as this is purely a guide to the Anglophones buried in the English Cemetery, I have not written about the foreign or French nationals unless they, their spouses or children have Anglo-American connections. This does by no means diminish their role within the Anglo-Protestant community, as indeed we know that many had very positive interactions within the *Colonie anglaise*. Purely for the purpose of reference their graves are listed in blue italics.

Unless otherwise stated, all photographs of the graves are my own work.

*

SECTION A

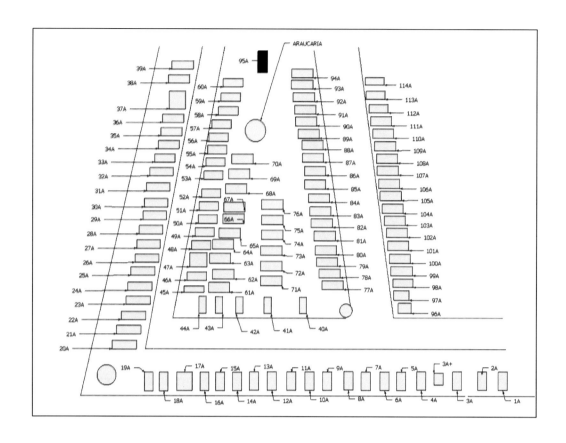

Grave	Name		Burial date	Age
1A	*OLIVIER*			
2A	*DORLEANS – LESCALIER*			
3A	*HAMON – HAUTE*			
3A+	*TREANTON, Albert (child)*			
4A	*BOSSARD*			
5A	*LEBERT – COROUGE*			
6A	**GRANGER, Alcime**	d. 11.02.1932	20.07.1932	52
	BELLEBON			
7A	**McCALLUM (Mac CALLUM), Frances Jane**		17.12.1932	89
	+ Edouard JEAN et Yvonne JEAN HAFFEN			
8A	*GIOFREDDO*			
9A	*LE GUEN*			
10A	**FREDERICK, Marescoe Lloyd**		03.11.1886	49
11A	**MOORE, Harold**	(d. 15.12.1947 – in Paris)	21.08.1948	52
	MOORE, Jeanne (née CHEDALLEUX)		11.09.1979	77
12A	**FILGATE, Marianne Alicia**		15.02.1886	27
	FILGATE, Martha (née MacCARTNEY)		02.03.1886	55
	FILGATE, Townley		05.05.1888	63

13A	*BERGEMANN – PIRO*		
14A	**ATKINS**, Clara Lucy	26.01.1884	66
	ATKINS, Emily Clara	15.12.1897	49
	ATKINS, Charles White	29.12.1897	79
15A	*HOUÉE – HAVARD*		
16A	**TROLLOPE**, Louisa (née PIPON)	21.08.1882	39
17A	*ROSAS – BRIOT*		
18A	**WREN**, Elise Valentine (née STOKES)	d. 16.06.1909	74
	WREN, Alice	11.04.1907	46
19A	**ALCOCK**, Anne (née KENNEDY)	09.01.1880	84
20A	**GEISTDOERFER**, Emma (née VADOT)	16.06.1930	44
21A	**JUMP**, Mary Shakespear	22.04.1870	74
22A	**SYMONS**, Evelyn (née WALSH)	25.06.1908	53
23A	**de SATGÉ**, Frédéric	23.02.1878	7 wks
	de SATGÉ, François	20.08.1883	15 mths
	de SATGÉ, Frances (née KNIPE)	23.10.1905	65
24A	**WOODHOUSE**, George Edward Leighton	d. 11.02.1960	70
	WOODHOUSE, Mary (née MANNING)	15.12.1960	63
25A	**BOUTON**, Charles Dumaresq	15.11.1877	53
	BOUTON, Henry Dumaresq	15.02.1888	30
	BOUTON, Julie (née BARRS)	27.02.1901	68
	LORRE / LEBON		
26A	**TAFFATZ – SOREL – NORDIN**		
27A	**GEORGE**, Catherine	04.06.1949	4
	GEORGE, Henri	d. 20.01.1970	80
28A	**BEISSAC**, Simone (née GEORGE)	23.06.1993	94
29A	**CHAUFFROY**, Marguerite (née GEISTDOERFER)	26.04.1954	77
	CHAUFFROY, Charles	06.09.1968	93
	CHAUFFROY, Alfred	13.10.1972	71
30A	**HARVEY**, Louisa Harriet	27.03.1876	45
31A	**GEORGE**, Jean Claude	16.07.1929	69
	GEORGE, Esther (née GEISTDOERFER)	24.12.1943	73
32A	**RAMES**, François	30.04.1927	64
	RAMES, (née GEISTDOERFER)	20.08.1947	80
33A	**DRAKE BROCKMAN**, Reginald Zouch	28.08.1875	5 mths
34A	**LOMBE**, Charles Evans	01.03.1875	47
35A	**DILLON**, Catherine Maria	13.02.1875	64
36A	**GEISTDOERFER**, Michel	25.04.1964	81
	GEISTDOERFER, Marie-Anne (née PICHARD)	26.07.1999	88
	GEISTDOERFER, Aliette	09.01.2015	71

37A	POWER, Frances, Lady (née WADE)	01.05.1874	61
38A	DICKSON, Linda	22.11.1873	15
39A	*BARTH, Charles (child)*		
40A	YOUNG, George Brook	24.05.1934	76
	YOUNG, Aileen Blanche	31.12.1935	41
41A	ATKINS, Charles Elton	09.04.1905	53
	ATKINS, Olivia	15.08.1905	52
42A	KALFF, Jacob	09.04.1910	54
43A	*BEZIE – BRIAND*		
44A	WREN, Leslie Robert	02.02.1910	37
	WREN, Ada	d. 14.04.1940	72
	WREN, Clara	03.03.1951	81
45A	DEANE-MORGAN, Flora Georgina,		
	Baroness Muskerry (née Skeffington)	23.12.1902	50
46A	BELL-MARTIN, Arthur Alexander Gonne	30.03.1883	57
47A	PRIOR, Benjamin John Chauvel	08.02.1886	55
	PRIOR, Diana Leybourne	15.05.1886	92
	PRIOR, Caroline	07.03.1887	90
	PRIOR, Sara Ann	01.05.1894	82
	PRIOR, Frances	15.10.1904	101
	PRIDEAUX, Mary Catherine (née MACLEOD	27.01.1936	76
48A	de COURCY CREAGH COEN, Hugh	29.10.1883	7
	CREAGH COEN, Nigel	28.04.1884	12
	CREAGH COEN, Violet Mary	28.04.1884	9
	COEN, Mary Frances (née ALKINS)	07.12.1888	44
49A	KINCAID, Charles Henry	15.02.1879	66
	KINCAID, Louisa	22.07.1884	69
	KINCAID, Donald	02.03.1912	68
50A	HARMAN, Avis / Avice Georgina	25.07.1899	15
	(HARMAN Rodolphe (at sea / en mer)	d. 28.07.1897	50
51A	BANNATYNE, James Millar	11.09.1898	65
	DELAUNAY, Adélina (née LEMIERE)	1907	77
	BANNATYNE, Adélina (née DELAUNAY)	06.07.1932	83
52A	PROCTER, Montagu Mitchell	08.10.1885	54
53A	CURTIS, Walter Henry Hamilton	16.11.1868	2
	CURTIS, James Charles	13.10.1889	69
54A	MORRISON, Walter	12.01.1890	68
55A	HOPE, Archibald Hugh	11.03.1890	70
56A	SULIVAN, Isabel Eugenia Henrietta	11.07.1900	31
57A	WAY, Arthur Dillon Cotton	16.12.1901	36

58A	BLACKLEY, Frederick	28.07.1890	48
59A	BARROW, Jacob	28.10.1890	81
60A	BARKER, Alice (née WRIGHT)	20.06.1891	57
61A	*COCHERIL – RICHARD*		
62A	*FAMILLE HUE – LEVEQUE –ELLIOT*		
63A	*LEFEUVRE – LEVREL*		
64A	*COLLET – DOHIN*		
65A	*ROUXEL – BOIVIN*		
66A	*LEMOINE – ARMANGE*		
67A	*BERTHELOT – LECOMTE*		
68A	*REHEL – MARCHIX*		
69A	*BENOIST – MEAL*		
70A	*CADES – GARNIER*		
71A	*LORRE – LE MAUX*		
72A	*GICQUEL – ROLLAND*		
73A	*LEFEVRE – DUPREZ*		
74A	*VILLALON – SILLARD*		
75A	*THEBAULT – COUDRAY*		
76A	*GICQUEL – ROLLAND*		
77A	*BRIAND – ABRAHAM*		
78A	SKIPPER, James Stark	03.03.1889	69
	SKIPPER, Emma Marian (née BRAUNE)	11.03.1903	65
79A	*DROGUET – VUILLE*		
80A	BULFORD, Agnes Lucy	05.10.1891	41
81A	de SATGÉ, Harriet (née ROWLEY)	26.07.1892	84
	de SATGÉ, Cosme Antoine	04.02.1898	57
82A	MILLER, Agnes (née MITCHELL)	25.08.1892	52
83A	PIERCE, Alfred Michell	12.01.1895	26
	PIERCE, Sophia Catherine (née SKINNER)	14.04.1897	62
84A	de SATGÉ de THOREN, Sinclair Ellis	22.01.1921	77
85A	ROBERTSON, Carey Argyll (née FRASER)	20.06.1924	73
86A	(plot removed from site)		
87A	HANNAY, Claude Patrick	21.11.1950	70
	HANNAY, Elizabeth Ellerton (née DORR)	05.10.1965	73
	HANNAY, Elizabeth Gwynn	03.07.2002	87
88A	SKEFFINGTON, Thomas Henry	22.01.1926	64
89A	SKEFFINGTON, Lily Elizabeth (née DEVOGE WILD)	02.07.1932	67
	SKEFFINGTON, Blennerhassett John	15.08.1935	69
90A	THOMSON, Lelia Douglas	28.02.1893	7 wks
	THOMSON, Emma (née VON ERICHSEN)	11.01.1926	72

91A	DOUGLAS LANE, Richard	20.10.1895	8½ mths
	DOUGLAS LANE, Genette	02.09.1898	11 mths
	DOUGLAS LANE, Lelia (née HOOKE)	07.12.1899	32
92A	HANNAY, Edmund	30.10.1895	67
	HANNAY, Martha (née GODBEY)	11.03.1899	58
93A	LEWIN, Jessie (née MACDONALD)	19.03.1893	35
94A	MACMULLEN, Mary	17.02.1953	
	MACMULLEN, Elizabeth	18.08.1964	76
95A	CAREY, Catherine		
	(plot acquired 1955, expired 1985, removed from site)	d. 06.04.1955	77
96A	TANDY, Gerald Dashwood	15.12.1881	1 mth
97A	BIRD, Maria Eularia (née CAMPBELL)	24.06.1924	86
	MEUNIER, Edith (née BIRD)	22.07.1963	98
	MEUNIER, François	20.11.1945	76
98A	MAIR, William Bissland	08.03.1873	40
	MAIR, Hermione Bissland	18.06.1876	19
99A	GORDON, Cecilia (née WALTER)	20.11.1872	49
	GORDON, Barbara Cecilia	10.12.1892	31
	GORDON, Robert	15.02.1893	67
100A	RINGLER THOMSON, John George	21.05.1872	48
101A	CONNOR, William Henry Brabazon	09.08.1871	63
102A	DOBRÉE, Harry	04.07.1871	73
103A	PERRYMAN, Edward	06.03.1871	78
104A	HILL, Augusta	20.01.1871	5
105A	SAUNDERS, Eliza (née CLEMONS)	20.12.1870	43
106A	HOLROYD, Charlotte (née JOHNSON)	d. 29.11.1870	37
107A	PIGOU, Cecil Henry	19.11.1870	14 mths
109A	DELAMAIN, Charles Henry	23.06.1870	77
110A	PARKINSON, Robert	30.05.1870	52
	PARKINSON, Caroline	24.02.1898	77
	PARKINSON, Marie Jeanne	01.06.1900	78
111A	COTHER, William	25.03.1870	57
112A	DUCKETT, Thomas Morton	14.01.1870	52
113A	O'BRIEN, Donatus James Thomond	06.09.1907	46
114A	ROPER, Margaret Emma	16.11.1869	16
115A	PYNE, William Augustus	20.12.1913	70
116A	GLASCO, John	01.05.1869	86
117A	WATSON, William Frederick Wilcocks	07.04.1869	51
118A	HOWES, Frederick	11.01.1867	47
119A	BROTHERTON, Manfred William Robert	10.05.1904	49

6A. GRANGER, Alcime (1879-1932).

Although a Frenchman, Alcime Granger's role in the latter years of the *Colonie anglaise* is of significance as he assisted schoolmistress Frances McCallum in the running of the girls' high school at *La Grande Vigne*. He had been severely wounded on the Western Front during the Great War.

7A. McCALLUM, Frances (1843-1932).

Frances Jane McCallum played a pivotal role in the realm of education for English-speaking girls in Dinan; she was headmistress of *Ker Even* and then *La Grande Vigne*, which later became the property of artist Yvonne Jean-Haffen (1895-1993), who chose to be buried in this same grave. Formerly headmistress of Woolwich Girls' School, she came from a teaching family and her sisters ran a school in Yorkshire. However, her brother Colin is best known as actor Charles Coborn (1852-1945).

10A. FREDERICK, Marescoe Lloyd (1837-1886).

Born in France to British parents, Frederick was a retired Royal Navy officer whose career was cut short when he was wounded aboard a warship and lost an arm. His grandfather was General the Honourable Arthur Grove-Annesley of Annesgrove House, County Cork. He married Cork-born Mary West (1845-1907) in 1874; the couple had children of similar ages to Cosme de Satgé's and the family is often mentioned in his diaries. They were living at *Villa Les Roses*, in *Rue de l'Amirauté* prior to his death. His probate records indicate he died at the *Chapelle Sainte-Catherine* in Dinan.

11A. MOORE, Harold (1895-1947) and MOORE, Jeanne, née CHEDALLEUX (1896-1979).

It is understood Harold Moore had served as a mechanic in the Royal Flying Corps, which later became the RAF. He married French-born Jeanne Chedalleux in Dinan in 1917 and Harold rented a garage in *Rue Thiers* where he worked as a car mechanic before building his own garage in *Rue Gambetta* in 1932. The couple lived in *Rue de la Lainerie*. Both he and Jeanne were interned during the German Occupation of Dinan.

12A. FILGATE, Marianne (1864-1886), FILGATE, Ellen Martha, (née MACARTNEY (1831-1886) and FILGATE, Townley (1825-1888).

Townley Filgate attended Painswick College, Cheltenham, before studying at Trinity College, Dublin where he was awarded a B.A. in 1848 and an M.A. in 1851. His wife and daughter passed away within days of each other and it could be that the family settled in Dinan because of the curative mineral springs at *La Fontaine-des-Eaux*. This grave houses his wife, daughter and himself.

14A. ATKINS, Clara Lucy, née ELTON (1817-1884), ATKINS, Emily Clara (1849-1897), ATKINS, Charles White (1818-1897).

Charles White Atkins came from a wealthy background whose ancestors had owned vast plantations in Jamaica; on reading Cosme de Satgé's diary and researching the family's movements, we discover that the Atkins had been in Dinan for a good while. Around 1875 they were renting *La Grande Vigne*. Atkins later became a church warden at *Christ Church Dinan*, the Anglican church. Buried here are Charles, wife Clara and daughter Emily.

16A. TROLLOPE, Louisa, née PIPON (1843-1882).

Edward Charles Trollope (1849-1904), a captain in the Royal Artillery, moved to Dinan for a short period with his wife, Louisa Sarah Pipon, a Jersey girl. Neither of them features in any of the census records, but Louisa, who died in Dinan at the age of 39, is buried in the *Carré anglais*. The couple lived in *Chemin de la Fontaine*; it is believed they came to Dinan for the mineral waters.

18A. WREN, Elise Valentine, née STOKES (*ca.* 1835-1909), WREN, Alice (*ca.* 1861-1907).

5 members of the Wren family are interred in two separate graves in the English Cemetery. Mother Elise and daughter Alice are buried here, both having passed away at the *Château de Saint-Valay*. Of Irish origin, the family's presence in Dinan during the latter years of the English Colony is well documented in *The Breton Briton*. In 1872 the family was living in Cabourg, Calvados.

19A. ALCOCK, Anne, née KENNEDY (*ca.* 1796-1880).

The daughter of the Reverend James Kennedy and Letitia Carew, Anne was born in County Wexford, Ireland. She married the Reverend Alexander Alcock (1788-1884) in Leinster in 1812. Her husband passed away in Saint-Servan in 1884.

20A. GEISTDOERFER, Emma, née VADOT (1886-1930).

Emma Vadot was the first wife of the politician Michel Geistdoerfer (1883-1964) (*cf.* 36A). Her striking tomb resembles a dolmen and the large flat rock was transported to Dinan from the Ile d'Ouessant (Ushant).

21A. JUMP, Mary Shakespear (1795-1870).

Very little is known about Mary Shakespear Jump, who died in Paris in 1870, other than that she had been a nun. Her parents lived in Tours for some years as their eldest son and three daughters also lived in France. Mary's niece Pauline went on to marry into the de Cargouet family of Lamballe, hence the Breton connection.

22A. SYMONS, Evelyn, née WALSH (1855-1908).

Erected in loving memory to my dear sister Evelyn, wife of Herbert Roland [sic] Symons who fell asleep July 1908.

Come unto me, all ye that labour and are heavy laden, and I will give you rest.

Originally from Dublin, Evelyn married Herbert Rowland Symons in London at Holy Trinity Brompton in 1881. They are mentioned frequently in the English-language newspaper *The Breton Briton*. Evelyn had numerous siblings so it is hard to say which one erected her gravestone.

23A. de SATGÉ, Frédéric (1877-1878), de SATGÉ, François (1882-1893), de SATGÉ, Frances, née KNIPE (1840-1905).

Left : Frances de Satgé. (*Coll. Nicholas de Satgé*).

The presence of the de Satgé family in Dinan between 1873 and beyond Cosme de Satgé's death in 1898 played a large role within the English Colony. This is the first of two family graves and houses Frédéric and François, two young sons of Cosme and wife Frances who is also buried here. Frances, née Knipe, was a doctor's daughter originally from Stratford-upon-Avon and married Cosme at Leigh Church in April 1873. (*cf.* 81A for further information about the family).

24A. WOODHOUSE, George Edward Leighton (1890-1960), WOODHOUSE, Mary, née MANNING (1897-1960).

Mary Manning, born in Nottingham, married George Leighton Woodhouse in 1919. It is of historical interest that in 1944, a young local Resistant Edmond de Blaye de Gaix (1926-1944) was executed by the Germans. Edmond was the brother of Marie-Louise de Blaye de Gaix who married Hilary John Leighton Woodhouse (1927-2015), son of the Woodhouse couple buried here and whose family still lives at the *Château de Landeboulou.*

25A. BOUTON, Charles Dumaresq (1824-1877), BOUTON, Henry Dumaresq (1858-1888), BOUTON, Julie, née BARRS (1832-1901).

Left: Photograph believed to be of Charles Bouton. (*Coll. B.M. de Dinan*).

The son of Philip Dumaresq Bouton, Jerseyman Charles lived in Dinan for most of his adult life; in 1853 he married Julie [Julia] Barrs in Jersey; born in Dinan she was the daughter of Captain George Barrs and Mary Ward (*cf.* 59B), pillars of the English Colony. Charles played an important role in the erection of Christ Church Dinan, the creation of the Victoria Club in 1868 and other societies. An erudite man and member of the *Chambre littéraire de Dinan* since 1852, he was also a talented artist and photographer and many of his sketches capture some landmark moments in Dinan's growth, such as the construction of the viaduct in 1852. He was also a freemason. The couple's son Henry, who was born in Dinan but served in the Royal Navy, is also buried in this grave as well as 2 members of the Lorre and Le Bon family who remained close to the Boutons.

26A. TAFFATZ – NORDIN – SOREL.

Four members of the Taffatz, Nordin, Sorel family are buried here. Their ancestor Ellen Trenchard (1842-1934) came from Jersey. The Taffatz family was originally from Switzerland and ran a successful pâtisserie in Dinan for many years which was held in high esteem by the English residents of the town.

27A. GEORGE, Catherine (1945-1949), GEORGE, Henri (1889-1970).

Left: Henri George at his house in Port Blanc in 1963. (*Coll. David Sellars*).

Henri George was the son of Jean-Claude George and Esther Geistdoerfer and was therefore the grandson of Jerseywoman Angelina Johnstone (the mother of politician Michel Geistdoerfer. (*cf.* 36A). Catherine was his daughter.

28A. BEISSAC, Simone, née GEORGE (1899-1993).

Left: Simone Beissac at Port Blanc in 1963. (*Coll. David Sellars*).
Simone was Henri George's sister. (*cf.* 27A).

29A. CHAUFFROY, Marguerite, née GEISTDOERFER (1877-1954), CHAUFFROY, Charles (1875-1968), CHAUFFROY, Alfred (1901-1972).

Middle Left: Marguerite Geistdoerfer as a child. (*Coll. David Sellars*).

Left: Charles Chauffroy. (*Coll. Patrick Geistdoerfer*).

Marguerite was the sister of politician Michel Geistdoerfer. She married cavalry officer Charles Chauffroy in Dinan in 1900. Alfred was their son.

30A. HARVEY, Louisa Harriet (1850-1876).

Probate records indicate Louisa died at *La Chesnaie* in Saint-Malo. Her brother was also living in France, near Combourg.

Lay up for yourselves treasures in heaven.
I know that my Redeemer liveth.

31A. GEORGE, Jean-Claude (1860-1929), GEORGE, Esther, née GEISTDOERFER (1870-1943).

32A. RAMES, François (1863-1927), RAMES, Angelina, née GEISTDOERFER (1867-1947).

Esther was another of Michel Geistdoerfer's sisters. She married Jean-Claude George in Dinan in 1888 aged 17. Angélina was also a sister of politician Michel Geistdoerfer. She married François Rames in Dinan in 1894. He was a *Lieutenant de Louveterie* and in Dinan had been elected to the *Conseil général.* Michel Geistdoerfer was a close friend of Rames and after the latter's death in 1927 he entered politics; standing for his late brother-in-law's seat, he won the post in the cantonal elections in Dinan that year.

Below left: Marguerite, Angélina and Esther Geistdoerfer. *Below right*: François Rames. (*Coll. Patrick Geistdoerfer*).

33A. DRAKE BROCKMAN, Reginald Zouch (1875-1875).

Stamp Duty receipt for Reginald Drake Brockman. (*Coll. Hugh Drake Brockman*).

Born in Camberwell, Reginald was the 5-month-old son of Alfred and Catherine (née Hart). The family may have been in Dinan for the curative waters at *La Fontaine-des-Eaux*.

34A. LOMBE, Charles Evans (1828-1875).

Charles Evans Lombe and his wife Josephine, née Hall (1826-1888) lived at *La Maison Blanche* in Quévert for a number of years. Their son Henry Joseph Buxton Lombe was born there in 1864. One of their daughters, Georgine Mabel, married James Cecil Balfour Craster (a resident of the *Colonie anglaise*) in Tichmarch in 1890. He died at Saint-Jouan-des-Guérets (35).

35A. DILLON, Catherine Maria (1811-1875).

Born in Queen's County, Ireland, Catherine Dillon, a spinster, died at *Place Duguesclin*. Her brother Charles Wellesley Dillon was in Dinan at the time of her death.

Blessed are the pure in heart for they will see God.

36A. GEISTDOERFER, Michel (1883-1964), GEISTDOERFER, Marie-Anne, née PICHARD (1911-1999), GEISTDOERFER, Aliette (1943-2015).

Michel Geistdoerfer's mother, Angelina Johnstone (1847-1912), although born in Ingouville, was actually from a Jersey family whose ancestors (Duchemin) were Huguenots from Tinchebray in Normandy; they had fled France and settled in Jersey at the time of the Revocation of the Edict of Nantes. Angelina was the niece of Esther Johnstone (*cf.* 54B) who had invited her over from Jersey to Dinan. A radical left-wing politician, Michel Geistdoerfer was mayor of Dinan from 1929-1940, deputy of the Côtes du Nord from 1928-1940, a Resistance fighter and the founder and editor of the newspaper *Dinan Républicain*. Re-elected in 1944, he was mayor of Dinan when it was liberated from the German Occupation. He was awarded the *Médaille de la Résitance* as well as the *Croix de Guerre* for his active involvement in World War I. A street in Dinan is named in his honour. Also buried here are his wife Marie-Anne and daughter Aliette. His parents are interred in the main French cemetery. Although of Protestant background it can be noted that the Geistdoerfer family has been atheist for over a century. The large tombstone is a carved granite rock from Languédias and the bronze portrait is the work of French sculptor Emile Armel-Beaufils (1882-1952), a friend of Michel Geistdoerfer.

37A. POWER, Frances, Lady, née WADE (1814-1874).

Born in Ireland, Frances Wade married Sir John Power (1798-1873) at Kilkenny Cathedral in 1835. He was 2nd Baronet of Kilfane. Frances's brother Robert Craven Wade (1809-1898) was Justice of the Peace in Clonabrany. Frances was living in *Rue du Viaduc* when she died. Her brother lived in Dinan with his family during the mid-1870s.

38A. DICKSON, Linda (1858-1873).

Linda was the younger sister of musical prodigy Antonia Dickson (1853-1903) and of William Kennedy Laurie Dickson (1860-1935) who later achieved fame as one of the pioneers in cinematography in the USA. The family lived in the Dinan area for many years.

Erected to the memory of her beloved child Linda Dickson by her bereaved mother, 19ᵗʰ Nov. 1873.

40A. YOUNG, George Brook (1858-1934), YOUNG, Aileen Blanche (1894-1935).

Aileen Young (1894-1935) was the daughter of Captain George Brook Young (1858-1934) and Anna Filgate (1861-1925). The family lived at *Pavillon de la Vallée*. George had married Anna, a daughter of Dinan resident Townley Filgate, in Bengal in 1893. The inscription here informs us that Anna is buried in West Tanfield churchyard.

41A. ATKINS, Charles Elton (1852-1905), ATKINS, Olivia (1852-1905).

Charles and Olivia were the son and daughter of Charles White Atkins (*cf.* 14A.). Charles was born in Jamaica and moved to Dinan as a child with his parents and siblings. He married a French lady, Angèle Fouéré and lived in Lanvallay. Olivia remained a spinster.

An active parishioner at Christ Church Dinan, Olivia was accorded a memorial window in the church, designed in 1906 by the famous Jersey stained-glass master Henry Thomas Bosdet (1857-1934). The Atkins family was well-liked by Cosme de Satgé.

42A. KALFF, Jacob (1855-1910).

Born in the Netherlands, Jacob Kalff married Marie Althea Fole-Bulley in London in 1888. A Doctor of Law, he was also Attorney-General of Dutch Guiana. At the time of his death he was living at the *Château de Vaulambert* near Corseul. The large column rising from his gravestone is broken at the top. We do not know for certain if this was caused by damage or if it was intentional. During the Victorian era, broken columns were often used as a symbol of a life cut short, or the loss of the head of the family.

44A. WREN, Leslie Robert (1872-1910), WREN, Ada (1867-1940), WREN, Clara (1870-1951).

This is the second Wren grave in the English Cemetery (*cf.* 18A). It houses Elise Wren's son Leslie and his spinster sisters Ada and Clara Wren. Leslie was born in Nantes where his father Leslie Senior died in 1894. In 1911 the spinsters were living at *Le Petit Parnasse* in *Rue Beaumanoir.* Both are listed as Irish, but born in Caen. Ada died in April 1940. If we assume Clara had Irish (or even French) citizenship during the German Occupation of Dinan, meant that her residency in Dinan was not posing any political threat. Clara played a significant role in the Resistance effort as she concealed radio transmitting devices in her house for Resistance Fighter Constant Heurtier (1905-1998). Considering that her house was located opposite *Mont-Parnasse*, one of the main German headquarters, it was a very bold action to take.

45A. DEANE-MORGAN, Flora Georgina, Baroness Muskerry, née SKEFFINGTON (1852-1902).

Daughter of Chichester and Amelia Skeffington, Flora was the sister of Thomas and Blennerhassett Skeffington, also buried in the English Cemetery (*cf.* 88A and 89A). Flora married Hamilton Deane-Morgan, Lord Muskerry, in 1872. Both the Skeffingtons and the Deane-Morgans were landed Irish gentry, the title Muskerry listed in the Peerage of Ireland. Flora and her husband were living at *La Ménardière* in Taden at the time of her death.

46A. BELL-MARTIN, Arthur Alexander Gonne (1825-1883).

Mort de M. le colonel anglais Bell-Martin. — Un terrible événement a jeté cette semaine une profonde et douloureuse émotion dans la colonie anglaise, à Dinan.

Un officier supérieur de l'armée britannique, M. Bell-Martin, colonel de cavalerie en non activité, habitant rue Saint-Malo, quittait Dinan il y a quelques jours pour se rendre en Angleterre. Il était à la station de Bishopstoke, où se croisent de nombreux trains, et se disposait à venir s'embarquer à Southampton. Le terrain faisant défaut en ce lieu, des poteaux supportent d'étroits abris excessivement rapprochés des diverses voies. M. Bell-Martin sortait précipitamment du buffet pour regagner le train, lorsqu'il heurta contre un des poteaux et tomba sur les rails. Il fut broyé par une locomotive arrivant au même instant derrière lui. On le releva en lambeaux, nous assure-t-on ; la tête était séparée du tronc.

Cette station a déjà été le théâtre de pareils accidents.

Jeudi dernier, le vapeur de Southampton ramenait à Saint-Malo les restes du malheureux colonel.

Un de nos plus honorables résidents anglais, M. le major-général Mac-Donald était allé chercher la triste dépouille de l'infortuné colonel, dont l'inhumation a eu lieu vendredi matin dans le cimetière de Dinan.

De nombreux amis, s'associant à la douleur de la respectable veuve de M. Bell-Martin, ont accompagné le corps au champ du repos.

M. le général de Lajaille, commandant la 40e brigade de cavalerie, et M. le major-général Mac-Donald tenaient deux des cordons du poêle.

M. Bell-Martin avait fait la guerre des Indes et montré une grande bravoure en combattant la révolte des Cipayes.

Cet officier supérieur était venu habiter Dinan l'année dernière ; il avait perdu récemment un fils, et son intention était de se fixer définitivement dans notre ville.

Nature intelligente, généreuse et bonne, M. le colonel Bell-Martin laisse des regrets sincères.

Colonel Arthur Gonne Bell-Martin's first wife, Letitia Martin (1815-1850), was the heiress to a large Irish land-owning family. In 1847 she married Arthur Gonne Bell, who was from a poor family. In an unprecedented move for Victorian times, he took on his wife's name, Martin, by Royal Licence and was known as Bell-Martin for the rest of his life. The colonel died in a tragic train accident in Hampshire on his way back to Dinan where he and his second wife were living; his widow arranged for his body to be brought to Dinan for burial in the *Cimetière anglais*. Major-General MacDonald collected his coffin on arrival in Saint-Malo. The tragedy was reported in full in the *Union malouine et dinannaise* (hereafter referred to as *U.M.D.*) on April 1st 1883.

47A. PRIOR, Benjamin John Chauvel (1830-1855), PRIOR, Diana Leybourne (1793-1886), PRIOR, Caroline (1796-1887), PRIOR, Sara Ann (1802-1894), PRIOR, Frances (1803-1904), PRIDEAUX, Mary Catherine, née MACLEOD (1860-1936).

The Prior family's presence in Dinan spanned decades and their name appears on every census record until the start of the new century. Spinsters Diana, Caroline, Sara and Frances were the aunts of Captain Benjamin John Chauvel Prior, of the 33rd Native Infantry and in 1861 they were living in *Rue de la Vieille Boucherie* (the current *Rue des Rouairies*); when they moved house, they never strayed far from *Les Buttes*. Benjamin had married Adeline Hoseason (1857-1927) in India; after his death she remained in Dinan at *Villa Le Belvédère* for some time before returning to Britain. The death of Frances Prior, aged almost 101, was reported in the local press; the article reveals how she had never wished to know her own age, that her longevity (in the family's genes) was also attributed to a diet of chicken and fish and that she was one of the first subscribers of the *U.M.D.* Mary Prideaux, closely related to the Priors, moved to Dinan just after World War I when she purchased *Villa Lea Roses* (also known as *Mont Oiseaux*) in *Rue de l'Amirauté*. She too is buried here.

48A. de COURCY CREAGH COEN, Hugh, (1876-1883), CREAGH COEN, Nigel (1872-1884), CREAGH COEN, Violet Mary (1874-1884), COEN, Mary Frances, née ALKINS, (1844-1888).

Without doubt the grave with the sorriest background in this part of the cemetery: three children of the Reverend John Creagh Coen (1844-1916) all died in tragic circumstances at a young age: Hugh (7) was killed in a fall and his siblings Nigel (12) and Violet (9) drowned in a boating accident on the Rance which was fully reported in the French and British press. Their mother died in Jersey but wished to be buried with her three children in Dinan. John Creagh Coen suffered a new tragedy in 1894 when back in England: his daughter Ethel (1869-1894) committed suicide.

49A. KINCAID, Charles Henry (1812-1879), KINCAID, Louisa, née PIERCE (1815-1884), KINCAID, Donald (1843-1912).

Born into a military family in Madras, Louisa Pierce married lawyer Charles Kincaid in London in 1841. Their son Donald (a British national) was born in Quimper (Finistère) in 1843; he lived in Brittany for almost all his life and his parents for over 3 decades. Charles and Louisa were residing at 15, *Place des Cordeliers* when he died. Cosme de Satgé's diaries inform us that son Donald was a member of the Victoria Club.

50A. HARMAN, Avis /Avice Georgina (1883-1899), and memorial to: HARMAN Rodolphe, died at sea (1847-1897).

Avis (Avice?) Georgina Harman was the daughter of Rodolphe Harman, brigade-surgeon-lieutenant-colonel in the British Army in India, and Ada Blennerhassett Skeffington (1854-1923), daughter of Chichester Skeffington and sister to Lady Muskerry (*cf.* 45A), Blennerhasset (*cf.* 89A) and Thomas Skeffington (*cf.* 88A). The stone also acts as a memorial to her father who died at sea on July 28th 1897.

51A. BANNATYNE, James Millar (1832-1898), DELAUNAY, Adélina, née LEMIERE (1830-1907), BANNATYNE, Adélina, née DELAUNAY (1848-1932).

Glaswegian James Millar Bannatyne was the son of Andrew Bannatyne L.L.D. and Margaret Millar. Also buried here are his French wife Adélina, and her mother, also named Adélina. James Bannatyne's residence at the time of his death was *Chalet Ille-et-Rance* at Léhon, although we know he had also resided at *Villa Gantrée* near Lamballe.

52A. PROCTER, Montagu Mitchell (1842-1885).

Les Réhories.
(Coll. Bibliothèque municipale de Dinan).

According to the obituary published in the local press, Major-General Montagu Mitchell Procter, of the Her Majesty's Bengal Staff Corps, died suddenly at his residence, *Les Réhories*, a villa which was frequently rented to the British. He married Ann Forrest in West Bengal in 1857. She was the sister of another member of the English Colony in Dinan, Robert Treston Forrest. Of note is that Montagu's father was the English poet Bryan Waller Procter (1787-1874), a friend of Lord Byron, who wrote poetry and drama under the pseudonym Barry Cornwall.

53A. CURTIS, Walter Henry Hamilton (1866-1868), CURTIS, James Charles (1820-1889).

Colonel James Curtis of Her Majesty's Bengal Staff Corps met his wife Harriet Hamilton (1834-1913) in India. He served in the Bengal Army from 1841 to 1868 and his own diaries contain details of camp life and marches in various parts of northern and central India, 1842-1849. These diaries and related records are held at the British Library, London. He died in Lanvallay; the family had lived in and near Dinan for many years and two of his daughters were educated in Dinan. Son Walter died in Dinan at the age of 2.

54A. MORRISON, Walter (1822-1890).

Left: La Redoute.

A retired lieutenant-colonel in the British Army, Walter Morrison was born in Cupar, Fife. He served on the Committee of the Victoria Club for a number of years. He was living at *La Redoute* at the time of his death.

55A. HOPE, Archibald Hugh (1820-1890).

Archibald Hope was a retired Major-General of the Madras Cavalry of Her Majesty's Indian Army. Born in Calcutta, he married Caroline Jones (1821-1912) in Bombay in 1842. An active member within the *Colonie anglaise*, he was on the committee of the Victoria Club, organised charity concerts and was church-warden at Christ Church Dinan. Cosme de Satgé became his successor.

56A. SULIVAN, Isabel Eugenia Henrietta (1869-1900).

Isabel Sulivan was the daughter of Rear-Admiral Thomas Baker Martin Sulivan (1826-1906) and his wife Isabel Cristina Victorina Dubose (1840-1927). The Sulivans were very active within the Colony and Isabel's father was even elected committee member of the *Société des Eaux* in 1896. He became church warden at Christ Church in 1897. The family often hosted very lavish balls, inviting French Dragoons and Hussars as guests, probably in the hope of marrying off some of the British girls, and one such party is referred to by author Gabriel-Louis Pringué in his work *Portraits et Fantômes*. Isabel's gravestone features a reference to St Patrick and honouring the dead, dated March 17th 1900.

57A. WAY, Arthur Dillon Cotton (1865-1901).

Grand Hôtel de Paris et d'Angleterre. (*Author's coll.*).

Born in Bombay, Arthur was the son of Major Alfred Cotton Way (1830-1871). In 1881 we find 15-year-old Arthur living at Rockhampton Villa, Jersey with his widowed mother and siblings. He went on to become Assistant Police Inspector in West Molesey. He died at the *Grand Hôtel d'Angleterre* in Dinan.

58A. BLACKLEY, Frederick (1842-1890).

Frederick Blackley was staying with his brother John in Lanvallay when he died. Born in Brussels, Frederick pursued a military career and reached the rank of lieutenant-colonel. He was based at Aldershot Barracks in 1871. His brother was also in the army. In 1879 we discover he was a freemason, initiated into the Ryde Lodge, Isle of Wight. It is fully possible he was a member of the British Lodge in Dinan, located in *Rue de la Mittrie.*

59A. BARROW, Jacob (1809-1890).

La Foresterie, Léhon. (*Author's coll.*).

Jacob Barrow was the brother of Major General Joseph Lyon Barrow (1812-1890), who lived at *La Foresterie* in Léhon with his second wife Emily McMaster and eleven of his fifteen children. Jacob died at *Place Duguesclin.* The family was of Jewish descent on both sides; Jacob's mother, Tryphena de Symons (1789-1828), was buried in the Sephardic Cemetery in London. After her death, widower Simon Barrow converted to Christianity, enabling him to enter politics and to place his sons in the Army, the Anglican Church, the law and medicine. Jacob, as we can see, was given an Anglican burial.

60A. BARKER, Alice, née WRIGHT (1833-1891).

Alice was born in Lincolnshire; she married Arthur Alcock Barker (1820-1897) in 1862. He was the rector of the parish of East Bridgford for 37 years and is buried there. Alice died in *Rue de l'Espérance*, perhaps visiting friends in Dinan. The inscription on her grave also pays tribute to her husband, now a widower.

78A. SKIPPER, James Stark (1819-1889), SKIPPER, Emma Marian, née BRAUNE (1836-1903).

Monte Casini. (Photo: François Cauwel).

James Skipper was born at Thorpe in Norwich and became a solicitor; some sources indicate he had been a corn merchant and also manager at the Norwich Equitable Fire Office. His third wife was Emma Marian Braune, eldest daughter of the Rev. G. Braune, Vicar of Wistowe, whom he married in 1874; she was the granddaughter of Admiral Sir Lawrence Halsted, K.C.B. and the Hon. Lady Halsted, daughter of Lord Exmouth. James Stark Skipper died at *Monte Casini* in *Rue Beaumanoir*. His widow later moved to Dinard where she died at *Chalet Clairette*. Her probate was handled by the Rev. Charles Seagrim (1865-1927), chaplain at Christ Church Dinan. It is interesting to note that the Skippers were related to the Barrow family (*cf.* 59A).

80A. BULFORD, Agnes Lucy (1850-1891).

Agnes Lucy's father was Edmund Bulford who was born in Dinan in 1825. He was one of several Bulford siblings to have been born and raised in the English Colony of Dinan, the children of John Bulford and Mary Ann, née Lynch (*cf.* 43B). Agnes previously worked as a governess in Britain and was now living in *Rue Thiers*. Her other sisters are buried in grave 44B.

81A. de SATGÉ, Harriet, née ROWLEY (1808-1892), de SATGÉ, Cosme Antoine (1840-1898).

Far left: Rare glass plate of Cosme de Satgé's grave, taken by Auguste Dubois shortly after de Satgé's death in 1898.

(*Coll. Bibliothèque municipale de Dinan*).

Cosme and Harriet de Satgé. (*Coll. Nicholas de Satgè*).

The Honourable Harriet de Satgé, great-niece of the Duke of Wellington and daughter of Irish landowner Clotworthy Rowley, Lord Langford of Summerhill (1763-1825), was the mother of Cosme de Satgé who is buried here with her. His diaries are an invaluable historical legacy as for the very first time we have live streaming written by a member of the *Colonie anglaise* of Dinan, who in spite of being a French national, was the husband of an Englishwoman who did not speak fluent French. Cosme was totally bilingual, a qualified lawyer, a devout churchgoer, devoted father and became an elected Republican *Conseiller municipal* in Dinan. His presence at the core of the English Colony was highly important and became increasingly necessary: he was their French mouthpiece, their translator and their intermediary when there were issues or problems. Highly esteemed by both the French and English, he proved to be the perfect diplomat.

82A. MILLER, Agnes, née MITCHELL (1837-1892).

In remembrance of Agnes, widow of Thomas Wilson Miller, Yokohama Japan, daughter of William Mitchell, Cupar, Fife, who died at Dinan, 22ⁿᵈ August 1892, aged 53.

Agnes Mitchell married merchant Thomas Wilson Miller in Japan in 1867. We know he was an active freemason in Japan and that he died there in 1871. He is buried in the Yokohama Foreign General Cemetery.

83A. PIERCE, Alfred Michell (1868-1895), PIERCE, Sophia Catherine, née SKINNER (1835-1897).

Sophia Skinner was born in Exeter. She married yeoman George Henry Pierce in 1858. Their son Alfred Michell Pierce was born in 1868. The family was living in Pleudihen at the time of Alfred's and Sophia's deaths, but had lived in the Dinan area for over 20 years. Sophia and George's daughter Marie-Louise was born in Taden in 1873.

84A. de SATGÉ de THOREN, Sinclair Ellis (1843-1921).

Left: Sinclair Ellis de Satgé de Thoren, photographed by Camille Silvy. (*Coll. National Portrait Gallery, London*).

Sinclair Ellis de Satgé de Thoren was the youngest son of Baron Oscar J. de Satgé de Thoren (1804-1904) who in turn was the brother of Cosme's father Antoine. Like Cosme, he was half-British, his mother being Millicent Wall (1807-1884). However, unlike Cosme, he received a very English education, studying law at Trinity College, Cambridge before entering the army. Here, he served for many years and is listed as Captain of the 5th Battalion of The Prince of Wales' Leinster Regiment (Royal Canadians). Sinclair, who had also worked as Professor of Military History and Tactics at Sandhurst, lived for some time in the mid-1880s in Jersey, firstly at a house belonging to his brother, Bellefield, and then at 31 Roseville Street, St Helier, where he prepared army students for military examinations, and along with some colleagues they named their school New College Jersey. Sinclair was also a well-loved socialite who was fêted by the rich and famous. He passed away in Dinard but chose to rest in Dinan where his family was living.

85A. ROBERTSON, Carey Argyll, née FRASER (1853-1924).

Left: Carey Argyll Robertson with the Princess of Cooch-Behar.
(*Coll. National Galleries of Scotland*).

Carey Argyll Robertson was the widow of the ophthalmologist Dr Douglas Argyll Robertson (1837-1909). During World War I she provided blankets and warm clothing for soldiers at the *Manoir de la Grand'Cour* and then rented another property, *Villa Le Belvédère* in Dinan which she converted into a hospital for the wounded. She was awarded the *Médaille de la Reconnaissance française* by the French government. She lived for many years at *Mont-Parnasse* with a companion, the Princess of Cooch Behar who is remembered for having worked as a voluntary nurse between 1914 and 1918. Her will, drawn up in Jersey in July 1924, cites her address as *Mont-Parnasse*.

87A. HANNAY, Claude Patrick (1880-1950), HANNAY, Elizabeth Ellerton, née DORR (1892-1965), HANNAY, Elizabeth Gwynn (1914-2002).

Left: Elizabeth Ellerton Hannay, née Dorr.
(*Coll. Debra Spiten*).

Left: Elizabeth Gwynn Hannay.

(*Photo: Groupement pour le service œcuménique des bords de Rance*.).

Originally from Cheltenham, Claude Hannay went on to marry American Elizabeth Ellerton Dorr; they lived in Mississippi where their children, including Elizabeth Gwynn was born. She attained the rank of major in

World War II and went on to become a very influential resident of Dinard who played a significant role at St Bartholomew's Church; It was largely thanks to her that as a pioneer of Ecumenism she worked to create the establishment of the *Groupement pour le service œcuménique des bords de Rance*. Elizabeth also founded the French branch of the International Ecumenical Fellowship.

88A. SKEFFINGTON, Thomas Henry (1862-1926).

Thomas was the brother of Baroness Muskerry (*cf.* 45A) and Blennerhassett (*cf.* 89A). In 1902 he was living in Taden. By 1906 we find him in Dinan at *La Vigne*, then at a later stage at *Villa Rosa* in the current *Rue de Coëtquen*. He and his brother Blennerhassett (known as Jack) had been planters and ran a small tea business in Dinan.

89A. SKEFFINGTON, Lily Elizabeth, née DEVOGE WILD (1865-1932), SKEFFINGTON, Blennerhassett John (1866-1935).

VENTE MOBILIÈRE

a Dinan, rue Lesage, villa « Jaclys », après décès de M. J. Skeffington, le LUNDI 9 Decembre 1935, à 14 heures.
On vendra notamment :
Lit de milieu avec sa garniture, autre lit a une place, chiffonnier, armoire penderie, armoire à linge, table marquetterie, glace psyche et plusieurs autres glaces, 2 commodes, banc coffre sculpté, plusieurs guéridons ou petites tables, lampes et bougeoirs, nombreuses gravures anglaises, commode ancienne, secrétaire, canapé et 2 fauteuils, travailleuse, bibliothèque, faïences anciennes, un poste de T.S.F. « Ondia », pendule de cheminée, petite pendule Boule, coffrets et nombreux bibelots, 2 sellettes, vieille horloge avec boîte sculptée, petit lustre avec cristaux, casier à musique, porte-parapluies, rideaux, tentures et tapis, 2 poeles, chaises, 2 tables à jeu, table et buffet de cuisinev, chaudron cuivre, théière cuivre, vaisselle et verrerie, 7 chaises de salle à manger, 2 buffets, table de salle à manger, outils de jardinage.
Et quantité d'autres objets.
10 p. cent en sus.
1 mois de délai.
— On visitera le Lundi 9 Décembre, de 10 h. à midi. 30-7

Union libérale, Novmeber 29th 1935.
Blennerhassett gained the rank of Lieutenant in the South Lancashire Regiment. He fought in the Boer War between 1900 and 1901 and also in World War I. He married Lily, the daughter of a Mancunian chemist, in London in 1900 and the couple settled in Dinan in the early 1900s. In 1906 we find them at *La Petite Vigne*.

Lily died at *Villa Jaclys* in *Rue Lesage* in 1932, her husband three years later. The executor of Lily's will was her neighbour, Miss Annie Nott (1882-1941), who was deported to La Flèche during the German Occupation of Dinan. Both Blennerhassett and his brother Thomas were active committee members of the Dinan Lawn Tennis Club.

90A. THOMSON, Lelia Douglas (1893-1893), THOMSON, Emma, née (von) ERICHSEN (*ca.* 1853-1926).

French-born dentist Noël Herford Thomson (1865-1943) lived in the Dinan-Dinard area for many decades and is frequently referred to in Cosme de Satgé's diaries. His first wife, Emma (von) Erichsen, was German; they wed in St Helier, Jersey in 1887. According to their marriage certificate she was 13 years older than her husband, quite an unusual union in those days. Their second child Lelia is buried here with Emma. Their first-born, Alice, was married for a few years to Ralph Maude (1873-1922), the editor of *The Breton Briton.*

91A. DOUGLAS LANE, Richard (1895-1895), DOUGLAS LANE, Genette (1897-1898), DOUGLAS LANE, Lelia, née HOOKE (1867-1899).

Lelia Hooke was the daughter of Thomas Brewer Hooke (1840-1898), one of Cosme de Satgé's friends. She married Charles Douglas Lane (1864-1931) on June 14th 1888, with a religious ceremony at Christ Church Dinan following the obligatory civil ceremony. Two of the couple's infants, Richard and Genette died young and are buried here; Lelia herself died in 1899. The Lanes lived at *Villa Saint-Paul* in *Rue Beaumanoir.* A memorial window was placed at Christ Church in her memory. Widower Charles remarried, his second wife was Vera Pellew Skipper (1876-1961).

92A. HANNAY, Edmund (1829-1895), HANNAY, Martha, née GODBEY (1840-1899).

Edmund and Martha were the parents of Claude Patrick Hannay and grandparents of Elizabeth Gwynn Hannay (*cf.* 87A). They lived in Lanvallay and were well acquainted with Cosme de Satgé and his family. Edmund was grated the honorary rank of lieutenant-colonel in the Antrim Artillery in 1876.

93A. LEWIN, Jessie, née MACDONALD) (1859-1893).

Left: Manoir de L'Echapt: Sketch by Henri Frotier de La Messelière, (*Coll. B.M. de Dinan*).

Jessie was the wife of surgeon Henric Lewin; friends of Cosme de Satgé, the couple was living at *Château de l'Echappe* (also known as *Château de l'Echapt*) in Léhon at the time of her death. The couple often hosted parties; Cosme mentions particularly the New Year's Eve gala at the Victoria Club in 1891.

94A. MACMULLEN, Mary (1886-1953), MACMULLEN, Elizabeth (1888-1964).

Mary and her sister Elizabeth were both born in Cork. Mary was living at 11 *Rue Saint-Malo* at the time of her death. Eleven years later, her sister's last address was 12 *Rue Chauffepieds*, a short stroll from her former residence. The sisters' brother Hubert was working in the tourism industry in Paris in the 1950s.

95A. CAREY, Catherine (1877-1955). *Plot acquired 1955, expired 1985, removed from site.*

Catherine Carey's grave was situated where the hedge and bush are now located. Catherine Carey was Irish and lived in *Rue de Léhon* at the time of her death. The lease to her plot expired in 1985 and was not renewed.

96A. TANDY, Gerald Dashwood (1881-1881).

Gerald was the son of Royal Navy Commander Dashwood Goldie Tandy (1840-1883) and Anna de Burgh (1850-1912). Dubliner Dashwood died suddenly in October 1883 when visiting his brother-in-law in Oldtown (Naas, Ireland). Anna Dashwood Tandy is often mentioned in Cosme de Satgé's diaries, as is her brother Thomas de Burgh (1851-1931). Anna and her eldest son Reginald (1883-1944) spent some time in Dinan in the early 1890s. Reginald became friends of the de Satgé children and later pursued a military career; he died in Jersey in 1944. (Westwinds, Tower Road, St Helier).

97A. BIRD, Maria Eularia, née CAMPBELL (1839-1924), MEUNIER, Edith, née BIRD (1865-1963), MEUNIER, Raoul (1869-1945).

Maria Eularia Campbell was baptised in Boulogne in 1842; the Dinan 1921 census suggests she was born in Dublin in 1839. She was the daughter of Robert Edgar Campbell, a captain in the Royal Welch Fusiliers. In 1861 she married Dubliner Henry Strathallan Trevor Usher Bird (1843-1880) in Bangor, North Wales. Their daughter Edith was born in Hamburg in 1865. Edith went on to marry Raoul Meunier. We know from various sources that Maria, estranged from her husband, lived at *La Billardais* in Taden for many years, but was residing at *Petit Beauvais* in *Rue des Fontaines* at the time of her death.

98A. MAIR, William Bissland (1832-1873), MAIR, Hermione Bissland (1857-1876).

Hermione was the daughter of William Bissland Mair and Jessie Innes Mair (1835-1918). The family had a strong attachment to the Dinan area as daughter Eveline was born in Dinan in 1867. The family lived in the *Haut-Bourgneuf* until William's death when widow Jessie moved to *Les Tilleuls* in *Rue de l'Espérance*. Jessie and her two spinster daughters Margaret (1858-1945) and Eveline (1867-1946) died in Dinard and are buried in the cemetery there.

99A. GORDON, Cecilia, née WALTER (1823-1872), GORDON, Barbara Cecilia (1860-1892), GORDON, Robert (1826-1893).

Cecilia was the second wife of retired Major Robert Gordon and the mother of Barbara Cecilia. The family had lived in Dinan for many years, firstly at *Les Caradeucs*. Barbara was living at *Villa Beauséjour* at the time of her death. Robert and his third wife Frances Treherne resided at *La Ville Goudelin* and then at *Mont-Parnasse*. Robert Gordon was also an amateur photographer. Eleven of his photographs of Dinan were exhibited at the Royal Photographic Society in London in 1876.

100A. RINGLER THOMSON, John George (1824-1872).

Very little is known about John George Ringler Thomson other than that he was born in Streatham, the son of John Ringler Thomson (*cf.* 16B) and Eliza Ann Round. He was admitted to a lunacy asylum in Middlesex in 1856, is known to have lived in St Helier. Jersey, and died in Léhon, possibly at the psychiatric hospital. Probate was only finalised in 1886.

101A. CONNOR, William Henry Brabazon (1809-1871).

NÉCROLOGIE.
— Les honorables résidants anglais de Dinan viennent d'éprouver une nouvelle perte dans la personne de M. William Henry Brabazon Connor, ancien officier de la garde personnelle de la Reine, capitaine de milice anglaise.
Le respectable M. Connor est très regretté de ses compatriotes. Il jouissait aussi à Dinan de l'estime et de l'amitié d'un grand nombre de Français.

U.M.D,
August 13th
1871.

Originally from Westmeath, Ireland, William became one of Her Majesty's Household Officers and Captain in the Militia. His second wife was Frances Scott with whom he had several children. After retiring, he lived at Draycott House, Kempsey, Worcestershire, before moving to Dinan where he died, at 21, *Place du Champ*. He was an esteemed member of the English Colony and highly respected by his French hosts.

102A. DOBRÉE, Harry (1797-1871).

Left: Harry Dobrée (*Coll. B.M. de Dinan*).

Below: U.M.D. July 9th 1871.

NÉCROLOGIE.

— M. Dobrée, ancien magistrat de l'île de Guernesey, est mort subitement à Dinan, d'un anévrisme, au commencement de cette semaine, à l'âge de 73 ans.

M. Dobrée habitait cette ville depuis longues années. Il avait été plusieurs fois nommé commissaire de la Société des Eaux ; il vivait environné de l'estime publique et de l'amitié de ses compatriotes.

Left: Beau-Séjour, the Seat of Harry Dobrée, Esquire. (Berry's *History of Guernsey*). The image dates from 1815 and dates from his father's time.

Born in Guernsey, Harry Dobrée Jnr was a retired magistrate of the island and had lived at Beau Séjour. He was residing in *Rue Neuve* in Dinan at the time of his death and was a popular member of the English Colony. The photograph of him (above) is from the Bouton-Barrs collection.

103A. PERRYMAN, Edward (1794-1871).

Edward Perryman was employed as the coachman to Major Charles Hamilton Fenton (1820-1882) who resided in the district of *Les Buttes*, Dinan. He was born in Sidmouth, Devon and married Mary Ann Parris in London in 1854. He is listed as a tailor on his marriage certificate. It is interesting to note that his death certificate states he was still working for the Major at the age of 78, even though the British census of 1861 refers to him being retired.

104A. HILL, Augusta (1865-1871).

Augusta was the daughter of Major General Eustace Hill (1830-1907) and Cecilia Wheatley Elliott (1833-1916) whom he married in Calcutta. Augusta was born in London. One of her brothers, Eustace, was born in Dinan in 1870. The family lived at *Place Duclos*.

105A. SAUNDERS, Eliza, née CLEMONS (1822-1870).

Left: Ambrose Saunders (1816-1884). (*Private Coll.*).

Eliza was born in Madras, the daughter of Major James Clemons and married Colonel Ambrose Edward Saunders in 1845 in Bombay. The couple was residing in the district of *Les Buttes* at the time of her death. Charles Dumaresq Bouton was witness to her death certificate. Ambrose passed away in St Saviour, Jersey in 1884.

106A. HOLROYD, Charlotte, née JOHNSON (1833-1870).

The daughter of Adolphus Johnson and Sarah Williams, Charlotte was born at Highgate, London; she married George Frederic Holroyd in 1862. Her death certificate indicates she was living in *Rue Saint-Malo* at the time of her passing. One of the witnesses to her death certificate was Charles Dumaresq Bouton.

107A. PIGOU, Cecil Henry (1869-1870).

Cecil Pigou was the son of Major General Arthur Comyn Pigou (*ca.* 1825-1902), a good friend of Cosme de Satgé and a very active member of the English Colony. He had previously served at Government House in Alderney. Cecil was the last of nine children of Arthur Comyn Pigou and his wife Jemima Norris (1823-1883). The family was residing at *Les Combournaises* at the time of the child's death.

109A. DELAMAIN, Charles Henry (1796-1870).

Sacred to the memory of Charles Henry Delamain Esq., Colonel, late in command of the Regiment of Bombay Light Cavalry and Companion of the Bath. Died on 19ᵗʰ June 1870.

He was the husband of Susan Sarah Christine Gun (1824-1888) and father of two sons who were born in Jersey and baptised at parish church of St Helier. An inscription on his gravestone suggests it was the work of memorial-maker E. Cochrane of Jersey. He was living at Saint-Servan at the time of his death but passed away in Dinan, in *Rue Beaumanoir*.

110A. PARKINSON, Robert (1818-1870), PARKINSON, Caroline (1820-1898), PARKINSON, Mary Jane (1822-1900).

Buried here are three unmarried siblings, all born in Calais to British parents, Robert Parkinson and Charlotte Chamberlayne. They were baptised at the Anglican Church in Calais along with their other siblings and all were British subjects. It is actually quite possible that these three never even visited Britain once in their entire lives. They are one of a number of cases of second-generation Britons who spent their lives in France, presumably bilingual. The Parkinsons lived in Dinan for a number of decades.

111A. COTHER, William (1812-1870).

The son of a surgeon, William Cother was born in Gloucester and was baptised in the Cathedral. He went on to become a barrister and married Marion Warburton (1830-1924) a doctor's daughter, in 1850. In 1871 Marion married widower John Goldsmith Orger, the chaplain of Christ Church Dinan. The marriage was celebrated by the Dean of Connor. Marion's cousin William Warburton, a Paymaster in the Royal Navy, lived in Dinan for many years with his family. Marion continued to tend to her first husband's grave and renewed the lease when required.

112A. DUCKETT, Thomas Morton (1817-1870).

Irishman Thomas Morton Duckett studied at Trinity College Dublin and became a barrister. He married Phillis Lucinda Strange (1820-1897) in Kenmare in 1849. In 1851 the Channel Island census places them at Richmond Place, St Lawrence, Jersey where one of their sons, William was born; he was baptised at the Anglican parish church of St Lawrence.

113A. O'BRIEN, Donatus James Thomond (1860-1907).

Born in December 1860 in London, Donatus O'Brien joined the Indian Army where he reached the rank of Major. He married Mary Rodgers (1869-1951) in Amritsar in 1891. We know of at least one of their children was born in India. He was living at *Les Combournaises* in Dinan at the time of his death.

114A. ROPER, Margaret Emma (1853-1869).

Born in West Stoke, Margaret was one of the daughters of Henry Roper (1800-1863) and Charlotte Pleydell-Bouverie (1824-1892). Margaret's maternal grandfather was the Reverend Hon. Frederick Pleydell-Bouverie (1785-1857), Canon of Salisbury. Henry Roper was Knight of the Chief Justice of Bombay

115A. PYNE, William Augustus (1843-1913).

William Pyne was a well-liked member of the English Colony, who frequently participated in social events and is often mentioned in various sources including *The Breton Briton*. His sister Florence (1862-1950) married Archibald Craster (1855-1919), a good friend of Cosme de Satgé. At the time of his death William Pyne was living at *Pavillon de la Vallée* in *Rue du Viaduc* with his wife Clara (1850-1932).

116A. GLASCO, John (1780-1869).

The most fascinating aspect of John Glasco's gravestone is the fact that the whole cross and base have been inscribed in French; this inscription relates the story of his life in France:

Ici repose Docteur Glasco, Irlandais, Chirurgien en chef de l'armée Britannique, né à Dublin 1780, décédé à Dinan, 27 avril 1869. Fait prisonnier à la bataille de Talavera, mais libéré par ordre de l'Empereur Napoléon premier avec louange à cause des soins qu'il prodigua aux soldats français blessés sur le champ de bataille.

This translates as:

Here lies Dr Glasco, Irishman, Assistant-Surgeon in the British Army, born in Dublin in 1780, died in Dinan on April 27th 1869. Captured at the Battle of Talavera but liberated on the orders of Napoleon I with merit for having treated the French soldiers wounded on the battlefield.

His death certificate was witnessed by two of the pillars of the Anglican community in Dinan, Charles Dumaresq Bouton and Logan Downes.

117A. WATSON, William Frederick Wilcocks (1818-1869).

Far left: Photograph of William Watson. (*Coll. B.M. de Dinan*).

By far the most influential chaplain in Dinan, William Watson was one of the founders of Christ Church Dinan and along with Charles Dumaresq Bouton and Logan Downes, he purchased the land where the church was constructed. A graduate of Emmanuel College, Cambridge, Watson became chaplain in Dinan in 1861. After his wife Mary died in 1866 (*cf.* 60B), he remarried local parishioner Isabel Howes, née Hollingworth (1828-1908), whose husband Frederick is also buried here (*cf.* 118A). Both Watson and Howes are buried next to each other.

118A. HOWES, Frederick (1819-1867).

Frederick Howes was the husband of Isabel Hollingworth who went on to marry William Watson. The son of George Howes (1772-1855), rector of Spixworth, Frederick was born in Norfolk and went on to study Civil Law at Trinity Hall, Cambridge. He was living in *Rue du Rempart* at the time of his death.

119A. BROTHERTON, Manfred William Robert (1854-1904).

The burial of Manfred Brotherton caused quite a stir in the English Colony of Dinan. He died suddenly of natural causes at his house, *Les Pommiers*, in *Rue Saint-Malo* on May 5th 1904. One would be wrong to say he was an exemplary parishioner. He rarely attended church, was twice divorced and his son Manfred (1899-1981) was born out of wedlock and had not been baptised; he married the child's mother, Augusta Hampton (1870-1961), three years later. One of Brotherton's sisters was Mary Scaramucci (1863-1939), a regular churchgoer at Christ Church. What angered the Brotherton and Scaramucci relatives was the fact that at the cemetery, the chaplain Reverend George Irby (1838-1910) had omitted a vital part of the burial ceremony, namely the committal. There ensued a number of angry articles published in *The Breton Briton*.

*

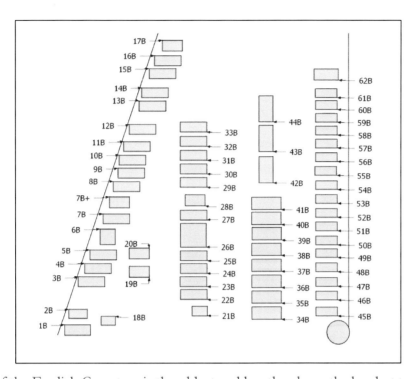

This section of the English Cemetery is the oldest and has thus been the hardest to chart. Because we lack the burial records prior to 1857, quite detailed research in situ has been required to ascertain the names of some of the occupants of each grave. It is largely thanks to old plans provided by the *Archives municipales de Dinan*, the impressive knowledge of the recently-retired *Gardien du cimetière*, Daniel Menou and a rough, but highly informative chart of Section B drawn up in the summer of 1893 by the Reverend Clement Sherard (1856-1927), a visiting cleric, that we have been able to compile this list.

Grave	Name	Burial date	Age
1B	ROGER, Emile	d. 09.02.1869	9
2B	LOCKHART, Norman Macdonald	d. 05.03.1853	73
3B	WISE, John	d. 28.06.1837	59
4B	CRASTER, Lockwood	d. 17.07.1834	5 wks
	CRASTER, William	d. 26.12.1836	1½ mths
	CRASTER, James	d. 17.09.1838	49
5B	MURRAY, James	d. 20.02.1838	71
6B	TILSTON, Rebecca (née FRANKS)	d. 02.02.1842	50
7B	IRVINE, Charles	07.05.1857	74
7B+	FONTAINE DE MERVÉ, Isabella (née GORE)	d. 05.11.1842	51

8B	O'BRIEN, Eugene	14.02.1957	83
	O'BRIEN, Mary (née THOMPSON)	18.04.1958	67
9B	MERRIEN, Elizabeth (née MERRISHAW)	18.03.1981	86
10B	STOW, James	d. 18.02.1844	68
11B	CLAPIN, Suzanne (née GUILLE)	16.06.1860	68
12B	KEANE, Louise Isobel	d. 26.10.1960	86
13B	HALLIDAY, Lionel	d. 26.01.1846	42
14B	SAWERS, Campbell	24.08.1866	50
15B	LEWER, Robert	d. 16.01.1847	51
16B	RINGLER THOMSON, John	05.03.1869	72
17B	BAINES, James Edgar	05.05.1903	63
17B+	SOUTHEY, Ida (née BIGGS)	d. 29.03.1958	87
18B	*LIETS, Louis (child)*		
19B	*SZWARCE, Emilie Julie (child)*		
20B	WILLIAMS, William James Pearce	d. 29.04.1842	3
21B	EBELING, Philip	04.02.1892	13 hrs
	EBELING, Winifred	04.02.1892	30 hrs
22B	SCHOALES, John	d. 25.07.1850	82
24B	BURNETT, Louisa Ann (née PARKER)	d. 19.06.1839	60
25B	PRENTIS, Catherine (née KNEVETT)	d. 01.08.1841	37
26B	CARPENTER, Richard	d. 15.08.1849	69
	CARPENTER, Sophia (née CROMWELL)	d. 20.08.1849	70
27B	HUGHES, Thomas	d. 07.04.1852	47
28B	EWART, Catherine	d. 29.10.1870	11 mths
29B	*SZWARCE, Emilie (née EKELT)*		
30B	*PLANTA, Monique*		
31B	PERCHARD, Anne (née Le Rossignol	d. 10.06.1850	57
32B	BURNETT, Louisa Margaret (née GRANT)	d. 29.11.1848	45
33B	GRANT, Ann (née WATERS)	d. 23.12.1853	76
	BUXTON, Margaret Annie	08.03.1862	21
34B	WOLLEY, Charlotte Elizabeth (née BISCOE)	d. 28.02.1851	39
35B	STEELE, Mary (née FISHER)	d. 11.03.1835	42
	MONTEITH, Mary Charlotte	d. 29.01.1851	9 days
36B	AYRE, Isabella (née GORDON)	d. 24.08.1855	56
	AYRE, William	21.01.1861	73
37B	DYSON, Elizabeth (née POLLARD)	23.03.1838	27

38B	JULIAN, Richard Archer	08.12.1860	30
39B	ROWED, Richard	05.02.1850	75
	ROWED, Elizabeth (née CARR)	29.04.1865	84
40B	PIERS, William Stapleton	27.12.1863	55
41B	STAINES, Elizabeth (née ROE)	d. 20.10.1850	49
42B	SURTEES, John	d. 08.12.1849	91
	(SURTEES, Harriet)?	d. 12.06.1881	76
43B	BULFORD, John	28.12.1859	76
	BULFORD, Mary Anne (née LYNCH)	09.08.1869	75
44B	BULFORD, Elizabeth	15.10.1889	69
	BULFORD, Rosa Jane	15.01.1918	94
	SEDDON, Emmeline (née BULFORD)	24.01.1929	90
45B	GARDINER, William	05.12.1860	14
46B	DOWNES, Arthur	14.06.1927	60
	DOWNES, Henry Noel	31.10.1929	78
47B	MORRIS, Mary Caroline	07.01.1862	16
48B	PRENTIS, Stephen	14.06.1862	61
49B	FAYRER, Agnes (née WILKINSON)	10.12.1861	64
	FAYRER, Robert	23.04.1869	81
50B	DOWNES, Ellen Ann	17.12.1861	13
	DOWNES, Logan	22.03.1873	56
51B	STEWART, Henry Brougham	30.09.1879	21
52B	DRAKE, Edward John	27.02.1863	63
	DRAKE, Julia (née MASON)	15.08.1883	75
53B	GEISTDOERFER, Jean	23.10.1935	66
54B	GEISTDOERFER, Esther (née JOHNSTONE)	22.08.1863	57
	GEISTDOERFER, Jean	d. 05.07.1876	74
	JOHNSTONE, Suzanne	24.01.1885	84
55B	THURBURN, Alexander	30.06.1864	59
56B	MACLEOD, Charles Beachcroft Hall	27.09.1864	10
57B	BLYTH, Edward Henry	14.03.1865	54
58B	BISSETT, George Edward Lawes Charles	30.03.1865	33
59B	BARRS, Mary (née WARD)	29.09.1865	60
	BARRS, Charles	10.09.1880	52
	BARRS, Emma Georgina	02.07.1912	81
60B	WATSON, Mary Jane (née FENNELL)	28.01.1866	50

61B	KITCHENER, Mary Emma (née GREEN)	14.01.1918	84
62B	CRASTER, Charles Herbert	14.08.1866	3
	CRASTER, Archibald Sinclair	11.03.1919	63
	MAGENIS, Florence Henrietta	22.11.1871	37

1B. ROGER, Emile (*ca.* 1860-1869).

Emile was the son of Auguste Roger, a Protestant minister labelled on the death certificate as *Pasteur Anglais*, and Elisabeth Levesconte living at *Les Combournaises* at the time of their son's death. In 1861 the family was living at *La Vigne* in the vicinity of *Rue Saint-Malo*. According to his death certificate Emile was born in Jersey. Auguste was a very active voice in the Protestant community is Dinan in the 1860s.

2B. LOCKHART, Norman MacDonald (*ca.* 1780-1853).

Left: Elizabeth MacDonald Lockhart (1735-1787) by Jeremiah Davison. (*Coll. The Company of Merchants of the City of Edinburgh.*)

Born in Argyllshire, Norman was the son of Charles Lockhart (1739-1796) and Elizabeth MacDonald of Largie and Muiravonside. Norman's father Charles legally changed his name to Charles MacDonald so that he could inherit title and arms after the death of his father-in-law. In 1805 Norman married Philadelphia (Phillis) Barbara McMurdo (1779-1825). They had 12 children. Phillis was a noted beauty and inspired several of Robert Burns' songs: *Phillis the Fair*, *Philly and Willie* and *Adown Winding Nith*.

3B. WISE, John (*ca.* 1778-1837).

The son of bookseller John Wise and his wife Mary Stacey, John Jnr was married to Mary Ellwood; the couple was living in the *Haut-Bourgneuf* at the time of his death.

4B. CRASTER, Lockwood (1834-1834), CRASTER, William (1836-1836), CRASTER, James (1788-1838).

The Craster family was one of the few whose presence in Dinan spans several decades; in their case it was seven decades. In the early 1830s we first come across retired lieutenant colonel James Craster, residing with his family at *Place du Marchix*, having lived in Dinan for around two years. He died in Dinan aged 49 and is buried here along with two of his infant children, both of whom were born and died in Dinan. He was married to Isabella Green (*ca.* 1805-1861). Other members of the Craster family are buried here too (*cf.* 62B).

5B. MURRAY, James (1768-1838).

James Murray was born in Dundee and was married to Isabella Dixon. The couple had also lived in the Netherlands where two children were born.

6B. TILSTON, Rebecca, née FRANKS (*ca.* 1792-1842).

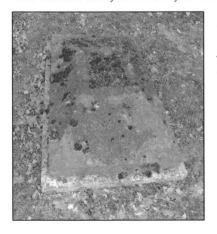

According to her death certificate, Rebecca was the daughter of James Hamilton and Rebecca Franks, and the wife of Joseph Tilston. She was born in Philadelphia, USA and died in *Rue Saint-Malo*. Unfortunately, we cannot gain any additional information from her gravestone as the metal plaque is missing. It strikes us odd that Rebecca's maiden name should be that of her (apparently) married mother.

7B. IRVINE, Charles (*ca.* 1783-1857).

Charles Irvine is the second person to be listed in the Anglican Register of Burials started by Reverend Richard Archer Julian in 1857. All we know from various sources is that he gained the rank of Major in the Royal Carabineers.

7B+ FONTAINE DE MERVÉ, Isabella, née GORE (1791-1842).

Far left: Photograph of Isabella, marquise de Mervé. (*Coll. B.M. de Dinan*).

Isabella was the daughter of Sir William and Lady Morris Gore and married Pierre Hubert Fontaine, marquis de Mervé, in London in 1827. He was the widower of Marie-Antoinette Laurent de Saint-Léger and had been one of the royal guards of the Kingdom of France. Isabella, a popular member of the English Colony in Dinan, died in *Rue Saint-Malo*. Her husband went on to marry another English-speaking lady, this time Mary Ann Mackenzie, a Catholic who is buried in the main French section of the cemetery.

8B. O'BRIEN, Eugène (1874-1957), O'BRIEN, Marie, née THOMPSON (1891-1958).

Left: Identity photograph of Eugène O'Brien. (*Coll. Archives départementales des Côtes d'Armor*).

Eugène was born in Ireland and moved to the USA where he fought in the Spanish-American War in 1898. He became a naturalised American citizen in 1902. For health reasons he moved to Pau in France and later to Paris with his London-born wife. At the time of his death he was staying in Dinan at 2, *Rue Thiers*, the house of his friends, Hyacinthe and Elizabeth Merrien (*cf.* 9B). His wife Marie Theresa Thompson died in Paris on April 18th 1958.

9B. MERRIEN, Elizabeth, née MERRISHAW (1895-1981).

Elizabeth in 1945 after the German Occupation. (*Coll. Anthony Merrien*).

Elizabeth married schoolteacher Hyacinthe Merrien (1885-1966) in West Deeping in 1924 before returning to her husband's native Brittany. Elizabeth took her husband's French citizenship. The couple lived in *Rue Thiers* in Dinan. Various records tell us that Elizabeth too was a teacher who gave private English lessons at their house. Considering the number of books which she donated to the English Library in Dinan, this comes as no surprise. In the 1931 census Mr and Mrs Merrien are listed as being the parents of two children born in 1925 and 1928.

10B. STOW, James (*ca.* 1776-1844).

The son of Daniel Stow, James was born in London. He married Charlotte Wright (1780-1849) in 1808. The family went on to have Jersey connections as his daughter-in-law Hermina Stow (née Waller) was living at Caesarea Terrace in St Saviour's Road in St Helier in 1866.

11B. CLAPIN, Susanne, née GUILLE (1791-1860).
Although there no longer remains any headstone between the graves of James Stow and Louise Keane, it is believed that Susanne Clapin is buried here. Born in St Ouen, Jersey, she married French army officer André Clapin, *Chevalier de Sainte-Hélène* in 1824 in St Helier. After her death he moved to Jersey where he died a year later. He was buried in St Martin's Parish Churchyard.

Le Sieur André Clapin, Huissier, Audiencier des Tribunaux Civil et de Commerce de l'Arrondissement de St Malo, né a Belan, Arrondissement de Chatillon sur Seine, Departement de la Côte d'Or, Veuf de D.lle Marie Cecile Jeanne Jehan, Fils Majeur de Jeus Mathieu et de Marie Morizot son Epouse, et D.lle Susanne Guille, née a la Paroisse de S.t Ouen, Isle de Jersey, Fille de Sieur Philippe Guille et de D.lle Anne Gasnier son Epouse, Jurent maries ensemble le Vingt-Deuxieme Jour d'Avril Mil huit Cent Vingt quatre.

12B. KEANE, Louise Isobel (1874-1960).

In loving memory of Louise Isabel [sic] Keane, late of Beech Park, Co. Clare, Ireland. 1874-1960.

The daughter of Perceval William Keane, Louise was born in Lislimnaghan, Tyrone, Ireland. She remained a spinster and was living at 35, *Rue Chateaubriand* at the time of her death.

13B. HALLIDAY, Lionel (1803-1846).

Born in Chertsey, Lionel Halliday joined the Royal Navy and was posted for some time around 1841 at Mont-à-l'Abbé, Jersey. He was married to Sophia Ann Noel. Three of their children were born in Jersey, another, Lionel Jnr, in Dinan in 1846, a matter of days before his own death.

14B. SAWERS, Campbell (1815-1866).

Born in Charlton, Kent, Campbell Sawers was a retired army officer who had served with the 69th Regiment of Foot Soldiers. In 1848 he married Jane Jessop-Brooke (1827-1918). At the time of his death he was staying at 3, *Rue du Château* in Dinan although he was ordinarily a resident of Southampton.

15B. LEWER, Robert (1795-1847).

 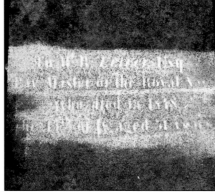

Robert Lewer was a retired Paymaster in the Royal Navy who had been living in the Dinan area for over 20 years with his French wife Eugénie Leroux and their 2 children. He died at *Le Petit Chatelier* at Saint-Samson-sur-Rance.

16B. RINGLER THOMSON, John (*ca.* 1797-1869).

Hôtel du Commerce. (Coll. Daniel Besnard).
John Ringler Thomson, born on the Isle of Wight, was the father of John George Ringler Thomson (*cf.* 100A). He was ordinarily a resident of Naples, Italy, but was staying at the *Hôtel du Commerce* in Dinan when he died. He married Eliza Round in 1823. He had connections with Jersey, as both his son John George and daughter Louisa (1825-1857) resided there for some time, the latter marrying Captain Thomas Hay Drummond in 1853. The 1861 census actually places him in Jersey. An esteemed visitor to Dinan, a full obituary was published in the *U.MD.* on March 7th 1869.

17B. BAINES, James Edgar (1840-1903).

James Baines, a retired lieutenant colonel in the Madras Army, divided his life between Guernsey and Dinan, where he lived at *Val Rive*. A close friend of Cosme de Satgé, his name appears regularly in his diaries. He was married to Mary Ann Eardley Howard (1851-1938). The gravestone also mentions the fact that Baines's son Kenneth (incidentally born in Sark) perished at Lille in January 1916. His daughter Mildred (1879-1954) married Thomas Clifton Hooke (1877-1942), the son of another member of the English Colony in Dinan.

17B+ SOUTHEY, Ida (née BIGGS) (1871-1958).

It is of note that the ossuary situated next to James Baines' grave now covers the site of the grave of Ida Southey, who was ordinarily a resident of Sables-d'Or-Les-Pins with her husband Henry. The couple had previously lived in India where they had a number of children.

20B. WILLIAMS, William James Pearce (1839-1842).

To the memory of a much beloved child, William J.P. Williams who died the 28th day of April 1842, aged 3 years.

William was the son of servant Thomas Williams and his wife Mary Ann, née Pearce. The child died at *Place Duguesclin*.

21B. EBELING, Philip (1892-1892), EBELING, Winifred (1892-1892).

Philip and Winifred were the twin babies of Dutch-born merchant Anthony Ebeling (*ca.*1842-1918) and his wife Grace Rosalie, née Woodhouse who was born in India. The couple married in India. Of note is that Anthony Ebeling became a naturalised British citizen in 1890 when living on the Isle of Wight with his wife and two daughters, Nora and Dorothy. The family was living at *Villa le Belvédère* in *Rue des Buttes* at the time of the twin babies' death hours after their birth.

22B. SCHOALES, John (1768-1850).

Mont-Parnasse.
(Coll. fam. Kergall).
Born in Londonderry, John Schoales went on to become a barrister. In 1801 he married Clementina Archer in Limerick and the couple had 9 children. He was widowed in 1849. It appears from his death certificate that he was staying at *Mont-Parnasse* in Dinan at the time of his death. His son, John Jnr (1810-1847) was instrumental in the immigration scheme on board the emigrant ship *Ganges* to Australia in 1841.

24B. BURNETT, Louisa Ann, née PARKER (1778-1839).

Louisa is one of a few examples of former plantation and slave owners who sold up and left after Emancipation. The daughter of plantation owner William Parker, she was born in Jamaica and married James Burnett, another plantation owner and the owner of a considerable number of enslaved people. After her husband's death in Jamaica in 1823, she continued running the plantation named after her, Louisiana. It is unclear when she moved to Dinan, although we know from records that other former plantation owners sold up and left Jamaica around the time of Emancipation and there are traces of a few others in Dinan. (*cf.* Atkins family, 14A & 41A).

25B. PRENTIS, Catherine, née KNEVETT (1803-1841).

Born in Ealing, Catherine Knevett was the daughter of Jonathan Knevett and Catherine Weeden. She married British poet Stephen Prentis (*cf.* 48B) in 1827. The couple moved to Dinan with their children in order for Catherine to take the waters at La Fontaine-des-Eaux: she was suffering from tuberculosis. Sadly, the waters did not cure her and she died in 1841. Prentis erected an impressive obelisk to her memory in the *Carré anglais*. Rather than move back to Britain, he remained in Dinan with his two children. His poem, *Oh! Think of me at times!* with the subtitle *Written in the Protestant Burial-ground* at Dinan, was published in 1841 in Dinan; this poem deeply expresses his love, his grief and his sense of loss.

26B. CARPENTER, Richard (1779-1849), CARPENTER, Sophia, née CROMWELL (1779-1849).

Buried in a very ornate double grave lies a couple whose death is shrouded in mystery. Richard Carpenter, born in London, became an active member of the Middlesex bench of magistrates. He married Sophia Cromwell in 1807. Of their two sons, Richard Cromwell Carpenter (1812–1855) became an ecclesiastical and Tractarian architect and is, I strongly believe, the designer of the splendid tomb of his parents. The circumstances of their deaths in Dinan are highly intriguing. Richard died in the district of *Les Buttes* on August 15th 1849. Elizabeth died six days later, in *Rue de la Lainerie*. They were buried in the *Cimetière anglais*, but not where they are to be found today. A document held in the municipal archives of Dinan dated September 1850 informs us in graphic detail that the two bodies were exhumed from their initial place of burial and reinterred in a new plot, presumably their current resting place. Their tomb is of exquisite beauty, their initials are carved into the stone and the edges of the twin graves are inscribed in Latin. This is clearly the work of a highly-skilled craftsman and is influenced by a Gothic and very high church hand, which would correspond well with the style of architecture their son was creating. To the visitor of the English Cemetery this grave stands out by its sheer ethereal and romantic grace.

27B. HUGHES, Thomas (1805-1852).

The starkness of this grave marks a sharp contrast with its neighbour, yet the occupant of this tomb was also exhumed from a prior location. Thomas Hughes was born in Boston, Massachusetts and was ordinarily resident of St Malo. In April 1852 he passed away at the psychiatric hospital of *Saint-Jean-de-Dieu* in Léhon and was buried in their cemetery. His brother had the body exhumed in July that year and reburied at this spot in the *Carré anglais*.

28B. EWART, Catherine (1869-1870).

Catherine was one of twin daughters born to Charles Bethune Ewart (1818-1903) and his wife Harriet Nicolle (1841-1933). Whilst Catherine died at the age of 11 months, Anna lived to the age of 101. Charles Ewart was a captain in the Royal Meath Militia and he and his family divided their lives between Jersey and *La Nourais* in Léhon. Over the coming years three more sons would be born in the Dinan area (1871, 1874 and 1876) and one in Jersey (1872).

31B. PERCHARD, Anne, née LE ROSSIGNOL (1790-1850).

Born in St Helier, Jersey, Anne was the wife of Nicolas Perchard, also from Jersey, whom she married in 1813. They had two sons, born in 1819 and 1823. Very little else has been found about her.

32B. BURNETT, Louisa Margaret Atchison, née GRANT (1803-1848).

Louisa was born in St Budeaux, Devon, the daughter of distinguished Royal Navy Lieutenant James Grant (1772-1833) and Ann, née Waters (*cf.* 33B). James died in Saint-Servan where he was buried. The family's presence in the Dinan area covered a few decades, and by 1866 Breton soil held the remains of four members. Louisa married Irish lieutenant Robert George Burnett in St Helier in 1838; his first wife and mother of his two daughters died in Jersey in 1836. Louisa and Robert were living at Brunswick Cottage, St Helier in the 1841 census. She died in *Rue du Coignet*, Dinan.

33B. GRANT, Ann, née WATERS (1777-1853), BUXTON, Margaret Annie (1840-1862).

Ann Grant was born in Chelsea and married Royal Navy Lieutenant James Grant in 1799. Margaret Buxton was her grand-daughter, born in Leicester in 1840 and baptised in Jersey in 1842. Her father was portrait artist Alfred Isaac Buxton (1804-1884). Her siblings James Fowell Buxton (1842-1911) and Florence (1848-1924) were also born on the island. Another brother, Alfred St Clair Buxton (1854-1920) was born in Taden.

34B. WOLLEY, Charlotte Elizabeth, née BISCOE (1811-1851).

The daughter of Joseph Seymour Biscoe (1761-1835), a graduate of Trinity College, Cambridge and lieutenant in the West Indian Regiment, Charlotte was born in 1811 in Clifton, Gloucestershire. Her grandmother was Lady Mary Seymour (1729-1762), daughter of Edward, 8th Duke of Somerset (1694-1757). Charlotte was therefore a direct descendant of Henry VIII's brother-in-law, Edward Seymour. She married Henry Wolley in Bristol in 1838.

35B. STEELE, Mary, née FISHER (1793-1835), MONTEITH, Mary Charlotte (1851-1851).

 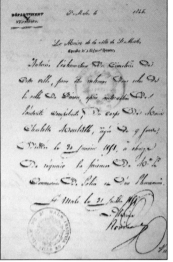

Mary was the wife of wine and spirit merchant Charles Hay Steele of Liverpool. She died in Taden; the inscription on her tombstone, commissioned by her husband, actually tells us more about him than her, but we do know she was born in Penrith and baptised at St Andrew's Church on February 14th 1793. In 1851, her baby grand-daughter, Mary Monteith, died in St Malo and was interred there, but was exhumed and re-interred with Mary in 1855.

36B. AYRE, Isabella, née GORDON (*ca.* 1799-1855), AYRE, William (*ca.* 1788-1861).

Originally from Devon, William Ayre was a paymaster in the Royal Navy; he married Isabella Gordon in London in 1821. The couple had been residing in Dinan for some time as William witnessed the death certificate of Louisa Burnett in 1848 (*cf.* 32B). They lived in the *Haut-Bourgneuf* area of Dinan.

37B. DYSON HOLLAND, Elizabeth, née POLLARD (1810-1838).

Elizabeth Mouse Susannah Pollard was born in Halifax. She married Cambridge graduate Thomas Dyson Holland (1810-1864) in 1832. The couple had at least three children. From the inscription on her stone we understand she passed away in Saint-Brieuc. Thomas remarried in 1843; a son was born in Guernsey in 1844 and we know of another born in Plumagoar in 1845.

38B. JULIAN, Richard Archer (1830-1860).

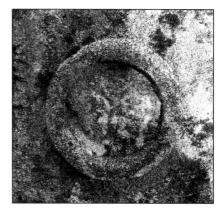

This exquisitely designed grave belongs to the Anglican chaplain Richard Archer Julian, who was born in Devon. He studied at Queen's and Emmanuel Colleges, Cambridge, was ordained deacon in 1853 and priest in 1855. In 1856 he married Mary Katharine Prentis (1829-1909) at the British Embassy in Paris – she was the daughter of British writer Stephen Prentis who was also living in Dinan (*cf.* 48B). It is understood that Julian was appointed chaplain at Dinan (and formerly at Coblenz) due to the fact that he was gravely ill with tuberculosis. The waters at both locations would hopefully alleviate his condition. Perhaps they did, but he nevertheless died in Dinan and was buried in the *Cimetière anglais*. It is significant that the only Baptism and Burial Registers we are able to consult were actually started by Julian; anything prior to this date has been lost. Julian begins both registers at number 1 in 1857. As well as a Christogram, the grave features a carved chalice and butterfly, symbol of Christian resurrection.

39B. ROWED, Richard (1774-1850), ROWED, Elizabeth, née CARR (1782-1865).

Richard Rowed was born in Caterham. Elizabeth was his second wife, and together they had a number of children including Richard Rowed Jnr (1803-1878), a good friend of Cosme de Satgé and an active member of the English Colony like his father before him. Richard Jnr was such an appreciated member of the English Colony that in May 1863 he was given, by way of gratitude, a painting and a silver tea set. Richard Snr and Elizabeth lived in *Rue de l'Ecole*.

40B. PIERS, William Stapleton (1808-1863).

William was the illegitimate son of the Anglo-Irish 6th Baronet Sir John Piers, whose sensational philandering had been the subject of an early poem by John Betjeman, *Sir John Piers*. William was born in Douglas, Isle of Man and with his wife Anna Maria Frances Baker (1815-1902), lived in *Rue de l'Amirauté* with their large family. They had been living in France for many years and married at the British Embassy in Brussels in 1842. They had 8 children, 6 born in Dunkirk and two in Dinan, a daughter even given the very Breton middle name "de Kervéguen". According to the *U.M.D.* widowed Mrs Piers left Dinan in April 1865 after having held a furniture and antique sale at her house.

41B. STAINES, Elizabeth, née ROE (*ca.* 1801-1850).

Elizabeth was the widow of Matthew William Staines, a Cambridge graduate who became a Protestant minister. They married in York in 1817. She was born in Bangor and was living in the district of *Les Buttes* in Dinan at the time of her death. It is believed that Stephen Prentis was writing about Elizabeth Staines in his lengthy essay, *Reflections in a Cemetary* [sic] *Abroad*, published by Huart in 1852 when he paid tribute to Néel de La Vigne, Anselme Michel and "Mrs S".

42B. SURTEES, John (1755-1849), [SURTEES, Harriet Allen (1807-1881)?].

Les obsèques de Mademoiselle Surtees ont eu lieu mercredi dernier, à 10 heures. Le clergé de la commune de Taden, dans laquelle est situé le château de la Conninais, a fait la levée du corps, qui, déposé sur un corbillard décoré de draperies blanches, a été dirigé vers l'église Saint-Sauveur.

Une foule considérable a suivi le funèbre convoi. Mademoiselle Harriet Surtees a été inhumée dans le cimetière de Dinan.

Heureuses les âmes qui, comme celle de Mademoiselle Surtees, quittent ce monde en y laissant de si profonds souvenirs de leurs bonnes actions!

John Surtees purchased *Château de la Conninais* in Taden in 1820. He was the first and only English property-owner in Dinan even as late as 1843. He was the wealthy young brother of the Countess of Eldon and rarely mingled with the other English residents; his daughters married upper-class / noble Frenchmen. However, we have a mystery: according to an obituary in the *U.M.D.*, his daughter Harriet who died a spinster in June 1881, was buried in the cemetery in Dinan, but there is no record of her burial in any of the archives and the tomb reveals no clues. Coincidentally, the status of her father's grave was upgraded to *Concession à perpétuité* on July 8th that year. So it is quite feasible that she is buried alongside her father.

43B. BULFORD, John (1782-1859), BULFORD, Mary Anne, née LYNCH (*ca.* 1789-1869).

NÉCROLOGIE.

La société anglaise de notre ville vient de faire une perte très regrettable en la personne de Monsieur le capitaine John Bulford, de la marine royale de S. M. B., décédé lundi dernier 26 décembre, à l'âge de 77 ans.

Ce digne officier, après d'honorables services militaires rendus à sa patrie, s'était marié en Angleterre ; en 1822 il vint se fixer à Dinan, où sont nés quatre des cinq enfants qui lui survivent.

Rien de plus respectable que la vie du *Captain Bulford* pendant son séjour de 38 ans dans notre jolie cité bretonne. Bon mari, bon père, cœur honnête et pieux, excellent homme sous tous les rapports, entouré d'une famille affectueuse et dévouée, à laquelle il a laissé le meilleur des exemples et le meilleur des souvenirs, il est mort dans un âge avancé, sans avoir fait un ennemi sur la terre.

Royal Navy officer John Bulford married Mary Anne Lynch in Exeter in 1815. Having reached the rank of Commander he retired and moved to Brittany with his wife and children around 1820; he received a full obituary in the local press. The family remained in Dinan for decades, mainly residing in the district of *Les Buttes.* In all. three generations of Bulfords lived in the town, some born there.

44B. BULFORD, Elizabeth (1817-1889), BULFORD, Rosa Jane (1820-1918), SEDDON, Emmeline, née BULFORD (1834-1929).

Elizabeth, Rosa and Emmeline were the daughters of John and Mary-Ann Bulford (*cf.* 43B). Emmeline was born in France and grew up in Dinan; she went on to marry the Pre-Raphaelite artist Thomas Seddon (1821-1856) and had a daughter Lily. Rosa and Elizabeth remained spinsters. They too were brought up in Dinan.

45B. GARDINER, William Wellisford (1847-1860).

Born in Hampstead, William died in Lanvallay, aged 14. He was the son of John and Alicia Gardiner.

46B. DOWNES, Arthur (1866-1927), DOWNES, Henry Noel (1854-1929).

Arthur and Henry were sons of Logan Downes (*cf.* 50B) who had played an instrumental role in the creation of Christ Church Dinan. Both men were born in Dinan. Absent from census records since 1886, it is believed Henry and Arthur lived abroad for many years and chose to return to Brittany later in life. Arthur died at the *Hôtel des Dunes* at Saint-Jacut-de-la-Mer. His brother Henry returned to Dinan where he resided and died at the *Hôtel des Voyageurs.*

49B. FAYRER, Agnes, née WILKINSON (1795-1861), FAYRER, Robert (1788-1869).

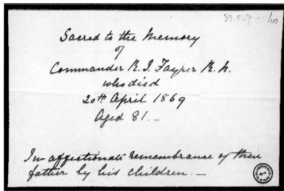

Left: Death announcement card sent to Charles Dumaresq Bouton by the children of Robert Fayrer. (*Coll. B.M. de Dinan*). *Below left*: Gold snuffbox of Commander Robert Fayrer. (*Coll. National Maritime Museum, Greenwich*).

Born in Heversham, Robert Fayrer joined the Royal Navy and reached the rank of commander. He later commanded the SS Liverpool's first transatlantic crossing in 1838 which the first by a two-funnelled paddle steamer. He was presented with a gold snuffbox on this occasion. He married Agnes Wilkinson in 1817 and they had six children. In 1851 the family was living in Jersey at Waverley Lodge.

50B. DOWNES, Ellen Ann (1848-1861), DOWNES, Logan (1816-1873).

Left: Logan Downes. (*Coll. B.M. de Dinan*).

Logan Downes was educated at Trinity College, Oxford and was one of the three founders of Christ Church Dinan. Logan married Ellen Scobell in 1847 and they had numerous children, some of whom were born in Dinan. The family lived at *Mont-Parnasse* for a number of years and also at *Le Poulichot* in Taden where he died. Ellen was one of his children.

51B. STEWART, Henry Brougham (*ca.* 1858-1879).

The Anglican burial registers note that Henry was an architect and lawyer in London. Born in Dublin, he was the son of William Stewart and Fanny Hogge. His brother William Neville, a businessman, was also living in Dinan, near the *Grands Fossés*, at the time of Henry's death.

52B. DRAKE, Edward John (1798-1863), DRAKE, Julia, née MASON (1808-1883).

— M. Edouard Drake, l'un des descendants du célèbre navigateur anglais, résidant à Dinan depuis une dizaine d'années, vient de succomber à la suite de douloureuses attaques de goutte dont il était atteint depuis longtemps.

We know from this couple's death certificates that they were both originally from Teignmouth in Devon. An obituary in the *U.M.D.* dated March 1st 1862 informs us that Edward Drake was a descendant of the Elizabethan navigator Sir Francis Drake (*ca.* 1540-1596). Julia Drake is referred to a few times in Cosme de Satgé's diaries and we know from Christ Church archives that she was a generous benefactor who donated £500 towards the building of the church in 1868.

53B. GEISTDOERFER, Jean Jacques (1869-1935).

Jean was the brother of the politician Michel Geistdoerfer (*cf.* 36A) and had three sisters, Marguerite (*cf.* 29A), Esther (*cf.* 31A) and Angélina (*cf.* 32A). Their mother was from Jersey. Jean was twice married, firstly to Marguerite Alix in Lille in 1906 and later in 1934 to Julia Meert in Saint-Cast.

54B. GEISTDOERFER, Esther, née JOHNSTONE (1806-1863), GEISTDOERFER, Jean (1802-1876), JOHNSTONE, Suzanne (1799-1885).

Far left: Esther Geistdoerfer, née Johnstone.
(*Coll. Patrick Geistdoerfer*).

In 1830, a young Alsatian aged 28, Jean Geistdoerfer (my great-uncle), arrived in Jersey. After having become acquainted with the Johnstone family, a protestant family of Norman descent which had expatriated after the Edict of Nantes, he married Esther Johnstone and came to live with her in France. In 1836 he set up a brewery in Léhon, close to Dinan.

These are the words of politician Michel Geistdoerfer, telling the story of how his ancestors from Jersey and the Alsace, now resting in this grave, came to settle in Dinan. Suzanne, who shares this grave with Esther and Jean, was Esther's sister. She died in *Rue de la Gare*.

Above left: Jean Geistdoerfer. *Above right:* Suzanne Johnstone. (*Coll. Patrick Geistdoerfer*).

55B. THURBURN, Alexander (1805-1864).

Alexander Thurburn was born in Banffshire, Scotland. He married Jemima Forbes (1806-1876) in Aberdeen in 1834. Five of their children were born in Alexandria, Egypt, where it is understood he was working as a merchant. He died in Lanvallay and his death certificate was witnessed by Charles Dumaresq Bouton and chaplain Richard Hunt Ingram.

56B. MACLEOD, Charles Beachcroft Hall (1854-1864).

Charles was the son of Surgeon-Major Alexander Macleod (1819-1914) and Sophia Purves Prior (1834-1867) who had married in India. He was born in India and was the brother of Mary Prideaux (1860-1936) (*cf.* 47A). Their mother Sophia Prior was the sister of Dinan resident Benjamin Chauvel Prior and the Prior spinsters whose lives furnished the English Colony's very essence for several decades. He died in the district of *Les Buttes* in Dinan.

57B. BLYTH, Edward Henry (*ca.* 1811-1865).

Edward Blyth was born in Britain and studied at Queen's College, Oxford. He lived in Jersey for many years with his wife, a colonel's daughter, Katherine Beckwith, whom he married in St Helier in 1842. Three of their children were born on the island. The family had close connections with France as Edward's father Samuel died in Paris in 1843. He was ordinarily resident of Windsor Crescent, St Helier, but it appears that he died at the hospital of *Saint-Jean-de-Dieu* in Léhon – his death certificate is witnessed by two of the religious brothers who worked at the establishment.

58B. BISSETT, George Edward Lawes Charles (1831-1865).

Born in Swanage, George served in the 55th (Westmorland) Regiment of Foot. He was wounded in Crimea in 1855 and ended his military career as Captain. With wife Elizabeth and daughter Florence they resided in the *Haut-Bourgneuf* district of Dinan. The insignia of his regiment is intricately carved by hand into the granite gravestone.

59B. BARRS, Mary, née WARD (1805-1865), BARRS, Charles (1828-1880), BARRS, Emma Georgina (1830-1912).

Left: Portrait believed to be of Miss Emma Barrs. (*Coll. B.M. de Dinan*).

Born in Bury St Edmunds, Mary Barrs was the widow of Captain George Barrs (1782-1833) who had been in Wellington's 33rd Infantry and fought at Quatre Bras and Waterloo; upon his retirement the couple moved to France. Son Charles was born in Caen and daughters Julie and Emma in Dinan. Captain Barrs was buried in the old cemetery behind the *Eglise Saint-Sauveur* as he died in 1833, prior to the existence of the new cemetery. Son Charles became a Paymaster in the Royal Navy. After George's death Mary set up a boarding house in the *Rue Saint-Malo* which she ran until her death. Daughter Emma, assisted by Julie and Charles Bouton, continued the management of the premises. Spinster Emma is remembered for having bequeathed a large sum of money to the *Hospice de Dinan* and her name appears on a plaque in the premises of the current town library.

60B. WATSON, Mary Jane, née FENNELL (1816-1866).

Mary Jane was the first wife of chaplain William Watson (*cf.* 117A) who is regarded as the principal founder of Christ Church Dinan. The couple married in Brighton in 1842. She died in the *Haut-Bourgneuf.*

61B. KITCHENER, Mary Emma, née GREEN (1835-1918).

Facing page, upper left: Mary Kitchener, photographed by Hughes & Mullins. (*Coll. Mme Nicole Lepage-Renault*).

Facing page, upper right: Manoir de la Grand'Cour, first residence of the Kitchener family in Dinan. (*Coll. B.M. de Dinan*).

Mary Green was the stepmother of Lord Herbert Kitchener; she had married widower Lieutenant-Colonel Henry Kitchener in 1866. They had a daughter, Kawara, who played a vital role in Dinan during World War I when she worked as a nurse to tend the wounded soldiers. Mary spent most of her latter years in Dinan where she was very active within the English-speaking community, organising social and religious events. She was a close friend of Cosme de Satgé's mother Harriet. The Kitcheners' first Dinan residence was the *Manoir de la Grand'Cour* at Tressaint; in the early 1870s the family moved to a townhouse, *L'Ancien Presbytère* in Dinan.

62B. CRASTER, Charles Herbert (1863-1866), CRASTER, Archibald Sinclair (1855-1919), MAGENIS, Florence Henrietta (1834-1871).

Charles was the son of James Thomas Craster (1831-1901) and grandson of James Craster (*cf.* 4B) and was born at the *Château de la Vairie* where his parents resided. The child died at Le Mans and his father had to seek permission to bring the body back to Dinan for burial.

Archibald was another of James Thomas' sons, who returned to Dinan to retire. He was one of Cosme de Satgé's hunting companions and often spoke to him about his tea plantations in Ceylon. He lived at *Villa Florence* in *Rue des Buttes*, where he died. It is of interest that the house was named after his wife, Florence Alice Pyne (1862-1950), sister of William Pyne (1843-1913), who also lived and died in Dinan. Florence Magenis was staying with James Thomas and his family at *Château de la Touche* near Dinan when she died.

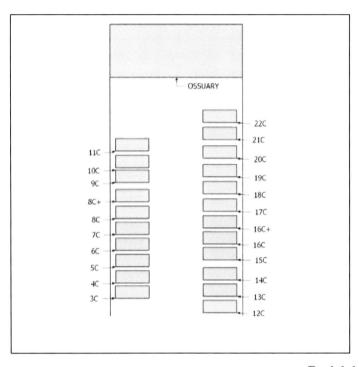

Grave	Name	Burial date	Age
1C-2C	*PLOTS REMOVED*		
3C	**WOODWARD, Charlotte Clara**	31.12.1907	42
4C	**ARTHUR, Henry Howard**	27.10.1911	64
5C	**GLENNIE, Isabella Maria**	09.10.1912	69
	GLENNIE, Harriet Mary	07.03.1924	86
6C	**ROSS, James Edmund Law**	17.02.1913	60
	ROSS, Harriet Jane (née AVERY)	26.10.1925	66
7C	**CUTHBERT, Alice Burn**	01.05.1913	60
8C	**GLENNIE, Elizabeth Anne**	05.09.1928	77
	GLENNIE, Margaret Gavina	11.03.1933	84
8C+	**FYFFE, Carnegie Susanna**	20.09.1918	63
9C	**BEOR, Elias Jenkins**	4.07.1921	78
	BEOR Elizabeth Harvey (née BELL)	d. 31.05.1922	73
10C	**HURLY, Maurice Randall**	d. 29.06.1927	63
11C	**TWEDDELL, Mathilde Josephine** **(née von DULCKEN)**	d. 05.12.1927	86
12C	**FORBES, Ella Gordon (née BERTIE CLAY)**	d. 01.02.1941	81
	FORBES, Sydney Muriel Gordon	20.12.1948	62
13C	**MACDERMOT, Evangeline (née SCOTT)**	d. 11.11.1940	82

14C	*DESTOUCHES*		
15C	SHUFFREY, Mary (née Dendy)	d. 24.08.1951	53
16C+	SMITHETT, Cyril Kingsmill	d. 29.07.1939	58
17C	BOUTON, Mary Louise	d. 04.07.1938	83
	BOUTON, Donah	d. 09.12.1960	94
	+ LORRE – LE BON		
18C	MAWER, Florrie	09.10.1929	35
19C	PARKES, Thomas George Ashforth	22.06.1929	66
20C	INGLES, Catherine Sophia (née GLENNIE)	14.08.1928	88
21C	VAUX, Edward Perceval	13.04.1911	65
	VAUX, Louisa (née HENTY)	21.09.1915	62
22C	KRAFFT, Jacques-Gustave	d. 20.11.1960	69
	KRAFFT, Christophe	d. 02.06.1979	56
	KRAFFT, Denyse (née de BOËRIO)	d. 02.03.1987	91

*

3C. WOODWARD, Charlotte Clara (1863-1907).

Born in London, Charlotte was the daughter of Oxonian Lionel Mabbot Woodward; she spent much of her adult life living with her widowed mother and siblings in the south of England. It is unknown why she settled in Dinan.

4C. ARTHUR, Henry Howard (1847-1911).

Born into an army family in Dublin, Henry Arthur reached the rank of Captain in the British Army. He married widow Helen Simons (née Whitaker) in 1890. They settled in Jersey and in 1891 were living at Oldholm, St Saviour. His probate documents indicate he was living in Dinan at the time of his death.

5C. GLENNIE, Isabella Maria (1842-1912), GLENNIE, Harriet Mary (1836-1924).

Isabella and Harriet were spinster siblings who, along with sisters Elizabeth and Margaret (*cf.* 8C) and Catherine (*cf.* 20C) had been dividing their time between Dinan and Devonport since the mid-1870s. They all played an active role within the English Colony and were friends of Cosme de Satgé's family. Their mother, Elizabeth Barker (1806-1889) lived in Dinan for a while and some books she owned can be found in the English Library. The spinsters lived at *Les Pervenches* in *Rue Beaumanoir* and later at *Villa Saint-Louis*.

6C. ROSS, James Edmund Law (1852-1913), ROSS, Harriet Jane, née AVERY (1858-1925).

According to the Christ Church burial register and the inscription on his gravestone, James Ross, born in Aberdeen, had worked for the French Cable Company. We know from the census records that James and his wife Harriet were living in Brest in 1906 where all the major cable work was being carried out. We also know that in 1901 James was naturalised French and the burial register also informs us that Penzance-born Harriet was naturalised French too, presumably through marriage. In 1913 they were living in *Rue des Rouairies* and later Harriet lived in *Rue Thiers*.

7C. CUTHBERT, Alice Burn (1853-1913).

Alice Burn Cuthbert

Alice was one of nine children born in Northumberland to William Cuthbert and his wife Mary, née Cookson. She was residing at 1, *Place Saint-Louis* when she died. A few of her books can be found in the English Library.

8C. GLENNIE, Elizabeth Anne (1851-1928), GLENNIE, Margaret Gavina (1849-1933).

Elizabeth and Margaret were the sisters of Isabella and Harriet (*cf.* 5C) and Catherine Ingles (*cf.* 20C). Both remained spinsters and lived at *Villa Saint-Louis* at the time of their deaths.

Left: Villa Saint-Louis.

8C+. FYFFE, Carnegie Susanna (1855-1918).

The daughter of Dundee ship chandler John Elphinstone Fyffe, Carnegie spent part of her childhood in Guernsey before attending boarding school in Dundee. She was residing at the *Manoir des Portes* in Pléven when she died. This manor is now the current *Mairie* (town hall) of Pléven.

9C. BEOR, Elias Jenkins (1842-1921), BEOR Elizabeth Harvey, née BELL (1849-1922).

 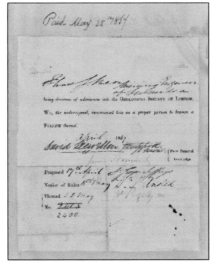

Left: Elias Beor's membership record. (*Coll. Geological Society*).

Elias Beor was a civil and mining engineer from Swansea, having obtained a PhD. He was elected a Fellow of the Geological Society on May 22nd 1867; he wrote a number of papers for the society. His resignation was accepted at the Council Meeting of May 3rd 1875, with no explanation for this. The Beors were living in Saint-Servan around 1920; Elias died at the *Asile de Léhon (Saint-Jean-de-Dieu)*, his wife a year later in Saint-Servan.

10C. HURLY, Maurice Randall (1864-1927).

Left: Grave plans drafted for the Hurly grave. (*Coll. Archives municipales de Dinan*).

Maurice Randall Hurly was born in Tralee, Ireland and studied at Cambridge. From the Royal Marines he joined the Indian Madras Staff Corps, reaching the rank of lieutenant-colonel; he fought in World War I. He married Honoria Fitzmaurice in 1896; their marriage was dissolved in 1907.

11C. TWEDDELL, Mathilde Josephine, née von DULCKEN (1841-1927).

Mathilde was the third daughter of Heinrich and Auguste von Dulcken; her two other sisters, Sophie (1835-1923) and Sarah (1836-1899) climbed to fame as musical prodigies, especially Sophie who married the Polish prince Wilhelm Radziwill. The family lived in the Dinard-Dinan area for a number of years. Mathilde married Francis Tweddell in Frankfurt-on-Main in 1862 and played a very active role in both the Dinan and Dinard English colonies. Her name often appears in the English-language newspaper *The Breton Briton*. This grave was erected by her children.

12C. FORBES, Ella Gordon, née BERTIE CLAY (1859-1941), FORBES, Sydney Muriel Gordon (*ca.* 1886-1948).

Ella was born into an army family in India and married Henry Francis Gordon Forbes (1850-1903)

in Bengal in 1875. Of her two children, daughter Sydney came to live with her in Brittany. They were living at *Villa les Hirondelles* in *Rue Gagon* when Ella died. Sydney died in Rennes. Ella was also the daughter-in-law (and Sydney the grand-daughter) of author Granville Hamilton Forbes (1825-1896) who is attributed by the British Library to have written *Britons in Brittany*, published in 1886 under the pseudonym G.H.F. Although we believe the author is related to Forbes, it cannot be said with any degree of certainty that the Cambridge-educated reverend was the actual author; he was aged 60 at the time and the author specifies he was a young man when the events of the book took place in 1885.

13C. MACDERMOT, Evangeline, née SCOTT (1856-1940).

Born in India, Evangeline attended boarding school in Britain. She married Irish surgeon Ralph MacDermot (1854-1918). Formerly residing at The Home of Good Hope in Bournemouth, she died in *Rue de la Garaye* in Dinan. Her daughter Margaret was also living in Dinan, both names are cited on a list drawn up for the occupying German forces.

15C. SHUFFREY, Mary, née DENDY (1898-1951).

Mary was married to Oxford schoolmaster Frederick Shuffrey (1896-1982) who had reached the rank of captain in World War I. Ordinarily resident of Uppingham, Mary died at the *Chauffepieds* hospital in Dinan.

16C+. SMITHETT, Cyril Kingsmill (1880-1939).

Although one record indicates that Cyril Kingsmill Smithett was buried in this grave with a lease expiry date of 2039, there is no stone, only a large blossoming hydrangea. He was born in Brighton and according to *The London Gazette* dated October 13th 1914, had previously served as lieutenant in the Queen's Westminster Rifles and was now in the 7th Battalion of the Duke of Cambridge's Own (Middlesex Regiment). He was ordinarily residing near Regent's Park in London. He died at the *Celtic Hôtel*, Saint-Cast, on July 29th 1939.

17C. BOUTON, Mary Louisa (1855-1938), BOUTON, Donah (1866-1960) (+ LORRE – LE BON).

Donah and Marie* were the daughters of Charles Dumaresq Bouton and his wife Julie (*cf.* 25A). They can be looked upon as the last true members of the English Colony in that they were both born to British parents and were brought up in Dinan. They remained spinsters and lived at *Bellevue* near the *Rue Saint-Malo*, a house their father acquired in 1874. It is touching to note that members of the Lorre and Le Bon family who remained very close to the Boutons, are interred in this same grave. Jean Le Bon, who died in 2016, spent much of his youth in the company of the elderly Donah Bouton.

* She disliked her English name and preferred to be known as Marie Louise.

18C. MAWER, Florrie (1894-1929).

Florence (Florrie) Mawer was a dental nurse who was ordinarily living at 60 Harley Street in London prior to her death at 12, *Rue Carnot* in Dinan. She died following injuries sustained from a fractured skull.

19C. PARKES, Thomas George Ashforth (1862-1929).

Banker Thomas Parkes was born in London, the son of an auctioneer. He married Estella Jost (1873-1941) in New York in 1896 and the couple settled in her native Canada. His probate records indicate he was still a resident of Nova Scotia at the time of his death in Dinan and we believe he died of peritonitis in *Rue Carnot*.

20C. INGLES, Catherine Sophia, née GLENNIE (1839-1928).

Catherine was the sister of the four Glennie spinsters buried in this part of the cemetery (*cf.* 5C and 8C) and was the widow of Rear-Admiral John Ingles (1842-1919) who died in Portsmouth but had previously lived with her and their children at *La Ménardais* in Taden. Of their numerous children, daughter Helen (1881-1962) became the second wife of dentist Noël Thomson. Another daughter, Mary Elizabeth (1869-1926), was born in Dinan. She became the wife of Admiral Cunningham Robert de Clare Foot (1864-1940). Mrs Foot, ordinarily resident in Wickham (Hants.), was staying at *Le Pavillon de la Vallée* in Dinan when she died in 1926. It is of note that Mary Foot's burial appears neither in the Anglican burial register nor in the cemetery's own records. We have not been able to locate her burial on British soil either.

21C. VAUX, Edward Perceval (1845-1911), VAUX, Louisa, née HENTY (1852-1915).

The son of a clergyman, Edward Perceval Vaux was born in Hertfordshire. He married Louisa Henty in 1886. They settled in Dinan in the late 1890s and lived at *Les Réhories* for many years. He replaced the late Cosme de Satgé as new church warden in 1898 and his name appears quite often in the correspondence and documents of the church.

22C. KRAFFT, Jacques-Gustave (1890-1960), KRAFFT, Christophe (1923-1979), KRAFFT, Denyse, née de BOËRIO (1895-1987).

Denyse Krafft was the daughter of Baron Henri de Boërio (1858-1917) and Constance Hooke (1864-1912), daughter of Cosme de Satgé's friend Thomas Hooke. She married the Swiss poet Jacques Gustave Krafft in 1921.

Those without Graves

Furthermore, we have a couple of individuals who died prior to the Anglican Church records (1857) and whose graves are listed on Sherard's cemetery chart of 1893 as well as the oldest chart at the *Archives municipales de Dinan*, but do not appear on the current map; their plot leases expired and the plots were either allocated to a new family or removed. We can be quite certain that these persons' remains are resting in one of the three ossuaries situated within the *Carré anglais*:

PORTER, Wilhelmina (née HILLARY)	d. 16.10.1851	41
DUSSAUZE, Nahomi	d. 10.02.1856	13 mths

(both plots removed from site)

Additionally, the Anglican Church registers indicate the burial of 34 English-speaking persons whose graves are not to be found in the *Carré anglais*. In the case of five of them, we know for certain that their grave leases expired and their remains were interred in one of the ossuaries and the plots re-leased or not used. Their transfer has been recorded.

BAKER, Alice Marianne (formerly 53B)	17.06.1861	12
BAKER, Mary Ann (née NICOLLE) (formerly 53B)	02.04.1863	44
PENNY, Caroline Annie (formerly 9B)	10.06.1868	16
PAGLAR, Jane (plot removed from site)	14.09.1872	59
MAUGER, Louisa Mary (plot included into ossuary)	26.06.1907	73

With regards to the remaining 28 on the list, we know from old charts and paperwork at the *Archives municipales* that they too had graves in the *Cimetière anglais* but their transfer to the ossuary has not been recorded. In cases where no prior grave location has been established, official documents such as the one accompanying Mary Giffard on her final journey from Pleudihen to the *Carré anglais* in 1862 do tell us she was once interred here. Whilst we cannot be 100% certain that their remains are in an ossuary, this theory seems the most plausible. These persons are:

HUGHES, Lionel Conway (formerly 12B)	24.10.1857	6
HUGHES, Sarah (née MACDONALD-JAMES) (formerly 12B)	12.06.1860	27
WILSON, John Alexander	23.07.1857	63
FENWICK, Louisa	26.12.1859	76
GIFFARD, Mary	21.06.1862	75

FAIRLIE, Cecil	05.03.1864	8½ mths
FAIRLIE, Ernest	20.03.1866	15 mths
PERRIN, Annie (née TAPSELL)	22.09.1866	33
AMY, Godfray (formerly 8B)	13.09.1868	36
CARWARDINE, Maria	02.07.1869	19
EDMONDS, John Salisbury (formerly 97A)	21.03.1873	24
EDMONDS, John Frederick (formerly 97A)	22.03.1877	60
REEVE, Mary Ann (née HUGMAN) (formerly 36A)	19.12.1874	74
TOOGOOD, Edward Brown (formerly 32A)	04.03.1876	45
LUTTE, Victor Edwin (formerly 31A)	18.03.1876	8 mths
FROST, Arthur Richard Nunn (formerly 29A)	14.07.1876	19
WILLIAMS, Ann Avison (née HOLT) (formerly 27A)	12.12.1876	45
HAMILTON, Isabelle (née DELAROCHEAULION) (formerly 20A)	17.01.1877	49
FAIRTLOUGH, Héloïse Marguerite (formerly 20A)	21.12.1879	17
REEVES, Thomas Burke (formerly 17A)	10.05.1882	40
BECKWITH, John Ferdinand (formerly 13A)	06.09.1884	60
WOODS, Thomas (formerly 15A)	26.12.1884	65
HOOKE, May Hilda Rose (formerly 77A)	26.08.1886	6
ELLIOTT, Charles (formerly 8A)	23.03.1887	60
CARBERY, Edward Spencer (formerly 7A)	26.05.1888	47
MILLER, Henry Edward (formerly 6A)	26.06.1888	55
LE VAVASSEUR DIT DURELL, George	19.04.1895	77
BELL, Margaret (née DAVYS)	14.10.1899	74

From this list, I feel it worthwhile to take a closer look at a few former graves:

1. **HUGHES, Lionel Conway (1851-1857).**

   HUGHES, Sarah, née MACDONALD-JAMES (1833-1860).

Formerly situated at plot 12B this grave housed the remains of Lionel Conway Hughes and his mother Sarah who was the wife of the Reverend John William Conway Hughes (1823-1887), the chaplain at Christ Church; Hughes had caused a major scandal in the community by writing love letters to a 13-year-old girl in the congregation. The scandal escalated to an even higher level when Sarah was found poisoned at their house at *Place Duguesclin*. The nature of her death at the age of 27 became public knowledge, even though no accusations were ever made against Hughes. Nevertheless, nobody wished to believe that the young mother of several children had willingly taken her own life.

2. **REEVE, Mary Ann, née HUGMAN (1802-1874).**

NÉCROLOGIE.

Une respectable dame anglaise, résidant à Dinan depuis plus de dix ans, Madame Mary-Anne Reeve, vient de mourir presque octogénaire.

Auteur de poésies estimées, cette dame s'était éprise d'une vive affection pour notre pays, qu'elle a chanté dans ses vers. Elle avait composé, il y a quelques années, un poème intitulé : « The Last of the La Garaye. » Cet ouvrage, édité avec luxe, et vendu au profit de diverses œuvres de bienfaisance, fut bientôt épuisé.

Sa santé étant devenue chancelante, Madame Reeve n'écrivait plus ; mais les bonnes œuvres continuaient d'occuper sa pensée tout entière ; aussi sa perte sera vivement ressentie non seulement par la colonie anglaise, mais encore par les pauvres de Dinan, qu'elle a si longtemps secourus.   F. T. C.

U.M.D., December 20th 1874.

Mary Ann's grave was formerly located at 36A. The daughter of travelling poet and artist John Hugman (1770-1846) Mary Ann became a poet too and published several works in Dinan including *Last of the Garayes and Other Poems by an Englishwoman* (1867).

3. **FAIRTLOUGH, Héloïse Marguerite (*ca.* 1862-1879).**

Formerly at 20A, this space housed the remains of 17-year-old Irish girl Héloïse Fairtlough who died on December 20th 1879. She was buried in the *Carré anglais* in the same grave as Isabelle Hamilton. She was the daughter of the affluent Thomas Fairtlough of Queensborough House, Drogheda. The Fairtlough family was still residing in Dinan in 1881. She died tragically whilst cleaning her gloves with petroleum which caught fire, ravaging her hands. The incident was reported in newspapers as far away as New Orleans.

4. **HOOKE, May Hilda Rose (1880-1886).**

May Hooke was the young daughter of Cosme de Satgé's friend, Thomas Brewer Hooke and the sister of Constance Hooke who went on to marry Henri de Boërio. She was born in Dinan.

5. CARBERY, Edward Spencer (1841-1888).

Barrister Edward Carbery was formerly buried in grave 7A. A retired British Guyana colonist who was fluent in French and German, he offered private tuition, inviting students to board at his house, *Ker Amiot* at *Les Buttes*, mainly focusing on those sitting the army examinations at Sandhurst and Woolwich.

Finally, we have the following French and foreign Anglo-Protestants who were buried by Christ Church but whose graves are not to be found in the *Carré anglais* either; it would appear that they too are now resting in the ossuary:

Georgina Rémy (1857, formerly 6A); Jacob Rech (1863); Axel Kjellestrand (1876); Louis de Coninck (1878, formerly 24A); Elisabeth Dufrêsne, née Soing – a French protestant who was the widow of a Catholic husband (1878); Gustave Dalton (1882, formerly 17A+); Elisabeth Barth, née Olgiati (1886, formerly 11A); Dominique Barth (1887, formerly 9A); Achille Oudinot de La Faverie (1891); Nicolas Soing (1894); Jean Barjeton (1909); and Elie Forni (1911).

Alexandra Letellier, née Robert, received an Anglo-Protestant funeral but was buried in the French section in 1933. We also know for certain that Baroness Marion de Ludwigsdorff who died in Paris on 29th October 1876 was initially interred in the *Cimetière anglais* (28A), but that her remains were moved into the ossuary on September 30th 1946. Incidentally, she was a good friend of the Bulfords and witnessed the marriage of Thomas Seddon and Emmeline Bulford in 1855. Swiss-born artist Ernest John Vulliemin died in Dinan on February 25th 1900, was buried in plot 43A; famed for his Peugeot bicycle posters of 1895 he also worked in collaboration with French author Hervé Bazin. There is no record of his burial in Christ Church's registers.

Of course, not all British nationals who died in Dinan were automatically buried here; there is the example of retired Royal Navy lieutenant Dudley Court (1850-1883) who died suddenly at his house at *Place Duguesclin* on October 19th 1883, but whose body was taken to Cherbourg for burial. Other families opted to have their loved-ones' remains transported back to Britain, such as The Honourable Arthur Caesar Tollemache (1797-1848), Lieutenant on half pay in Her Britannic Majesty's 6th Regiment of Dragoons, who died in Dinan on April 1st 1848 and was buried at All Souls, Kensal Green on June 16th that year, a cemetery which drew its inspiration from the *Père Lachaise* in Paris and was the most fashionable burial ground in Victorian England.

CONCLUSION

Although all this research paints a picture of how the English Cemetery once was and now is, we know that some people's former graves will never be able to be included in our list; the sad fact is that if there is no record of their burial in any of the archives, it would be hard to find those whose names are even unknown to us. Whilst researching another matter at the Jersey Archive, I chanced upon the will of Elizabeth Marianne Ireland, dated February 9th 1843. Research online led me to Elizabeth, née Mallack, who died in Dinan two days after signing her will, aged 59. Her death certificate was witnessed by her Dinan-based doctor, Frederick Pidsley and a certain William Downes. Attached to the will, held in Jersey, was a written statement by the Anglican chaplain in Dinan, Hugh Thomas Oxenham, confirming that Elizabeth Ireland was buried in the *Carré anglais*. This is probably the only record which tells us that she once was laid to rest here. The same can be said of Caroline Utting, née Williams, who died in Dinan on July 15th 1843, whose name features in a small notebook held at the *Archives municipales de Dinan*. Her death certificate was witnessed by the Reverend Peter Pering (1799-1886), cited as an Anglican minister.

This also indicates that there must have been others… and as we chance upon names in other fields of research such as Frances Law, née Willson who died in 1845 and Laura Pitt, a six-week-old baby who died in 1847, it makes us realise that this cemetery still holds its mysteries.

*

ACKNOWLEDGEMENTS

I would like to extend my thanks to all who have contributed to this work in whichever way, with a special mention to the following establishments in Dinan for their assistance with my research:

Archives municipales de Dinan – Véronique Riou – with independent input by Jean-Claude Cloarec.
Bibliothèque municipale de Dinan - Loïc-René Vilbert, Blandine Maufrais, Christopher Maurice.
Cimetière de Dinan – Daniel Menou, Jean-Jacques Saintilan.

*